SURVEILLANCE ZONE

SURVEILLANCE ZONE

AMI TOBEN

Surveillance Zone
© 2017 Ami Toben

All rights reserved. No part of this publication may be reproduced, stored, or transmitted in any form or by any means, electronic, mechanical, photocopying, recording, scanning, or otherwise, without written permission from the publisher. It is illegal to copy this book, post it to a website, or distribute it by any other means without permission.

 This book was designed by THE FRONTISPIECE. The text face is Mercury Text G1, designed by Jonathan Hoefler, with other elements set in Tungsten and Aldrich.

To Kathleen and David,
who are everything to me.

Table of Contents

Introduction

1. **Understanding Private Security & Surveillance**   5
2. **Who I Am**   13
3. **Inductive Observation: Watching & Understanding People**   31
4. **Hostile Surveillance**   41
5. **Mobile Surveillance**   51
6. **Hostile Surveillance Detection**   63
7. **Mobile Surveillance Detection**   73
8. **Lessons from the Field: Surveillance Detection**   81
9. **Lessons from the Field: Covert Operations**   91
10. **Surveillance Detection on Yourself**   103
11. **Circles of Security**   121
12. **So You Want To Be a Covert Operator**   143
13. *Conclusion*   153

All warfare is based on deception. There is no place where espionage is not used.

– *Sun Tzu.*

INTRODUCTION

San Francisco, 2015. It was still dark outside when the first undercover operative arrived at the Palace Hotel that morning. San Francisco, with its flair for the dramatic, set the scene for what was coming—a thick layer of fog swirled through the streets as the operative made his way into the lobby. He sat down on one of the sofas to wait for his partner, and for the man who had hired them for the job. The hotel was to be the site of a large tech conference that day, and the two operatives had to be in position fast. Conference attendees would soon be streaming in for registration, and before long, the guest speakers would begin to arrive—including one specific Silicon Valley billionaire they would be watching for.

As the hubbub in the lobby built to a crescendo, the operatives slid into the background, it was imperative for their mission that no one knew who they were or what they were doing there.

While this might sound like a nefarious plot in some Hollywood movie, let me assure you that it was nothing of the sort. In fact, it was quite the contrary. This suspicious-looking scene was actually a covert protective operation—one of many operations that I'll be letting you in on throughout the book—and part of a whole undercover world that very few people know exists.

The first undercover operative mentioned above was actually me, and the man who had hired us was the senior security director for a well-known Silicon Valley corporation. We had been brought in to covertly protect the billionaire founder and CEO, whose company—despite having experienced dramatic downswings and falling stock prices—was about to unveil some new ventures and technologies. This crazy mix of factors—combining angry stockholders, excited technologists, and nervous investors with billions of dollars on the line—is precisely what makes these high-voltage Silicon Valley situations so tricky and interesting.

On top of all that, the CEO had been receiving increasingly violent threats from an especially dedicated stalker who had demonstrated his willingness and ability to take things to the next level. Having surveilled the CEO's residence and workplace, and even physically confronted the CEO in these locations, there was ample reason to take the stalker's intentions seriously. When the threat to harm the CEO at the convention had come in (just a day before the event), the company decided to take action. At ten pm, I received a call from the security director, requesting our presence at the hotel at six am the following morning.

Providing "impossible" solutions for last-minute requests like this is a typical part of the crazy undercover world I live in. The CEO would have a covert security bubble around him the entire day. No one could know about it, because one photo, tweet, or post about him employing high-level security would have been enough to cause a sensation, further discouraging stockholders and warding off potential investors.

In order to maintain the illusion of normality, we were about to transform ourselves into tech conference attendees, hotel guests, maintenance workers, and personal assistants. We'd need to spread out and blend in—spending the day on the convention room floor, sitting in the front row of the lecture hall, standing backstage, waiting at the hotel entrance, hanging out in the alley outside the hotel, and running up and down dark emergency staircases.

I'd been in plenty of tricky covert operations before, but this one was going to be an interesting challenge...

ABOUT THE BOOK

I'll get back to our beleaguered CEO later. But first, let's take a step back. What exactly is this line of work and how much of it really takes place? Are we the "bad guys" who do the bidding of dark corporate interests? How does it even work? And how does someone like me get involved in it?

I'll answer these questions and more throughout the book, but I want to start by explaining what this field is and why I decided to write the book.

The story above is but a single example of the type of covert protective operations that take place every day in the private security sector. Over the years, I've found that most people don't even realize this field exists, and I've found two main reasons for this. First, most people in this field (including me, until recently) don't talk about their work. This is partly due to non-disclosure agreements (NDAs) that legally prohibit the disclosure of certain sensitive information, but mostly, in an industry of quiet professionals, it's considered bad form to talk too much. The second reason is that movies and TV shows have spun such outlandish tales about the work we do that many people just assume this field is entirely fictional and doesn't actually exist. And yet, as I will show you in detail, it most certainly does exist; it has for quite some time, and it's only getting bigger.

This is not another CIA book about spies and intelligence officers, or another exposé about overseas security contractors. Instead, I wanted to share a lesser-known story; to give you a glimpse into the mysterious world of covert protective operations that take place right here at home, right under most people's noses. Come with me, and I'll teach you the secrets of the trade. I'll show you how we do it and explain why you've never noticed us before.

A note on discretion and confidentiality: Although I'll be taking you behind the scenes of many undercover operations I've taken part in, no client details will be revealed in this book. You'll get accurate accounts of actual events, but I've taken great care to change various details so that the actual organizations and individuals involved will not be identified.

Having spent over a decade in this industry, and being one of the pioneers who helped develop it in the Silicon Valley, I think the time has finally come to share this story. Consider this your backstage pass, granting you access to this hidden world.

Let me tell you about the Surveillance Zone, and let me show you where it is.

I should warn you, however, that once you start viewing the world through this new lens, there's no turning back. You're about to discover that many of the conventions you're accustomed to, and many of the people you're used to seeing around you, are not at all what they seem. This book—should you choose to read it—will make it very difficult to return to the blissful ignorance you've lived in up until now.

No, this book will not self-destruct five seconds after you finish reading it, but now would be a good time to sit down and buckle up. It's going to be a crazy ride.

CHAPTER 1

UNDERSTANDING PRIVATE SECURITY & SURVEILLANCE

If you know the enemy and know yourself, you need not fear the result of a hundred battles.

—Sun Tzu, *The Art of War*

Before we delve into the fascinating world of private security—and take a look at areas like surveillance detection, protective intelligence, and covert protection—it's important to understand what these measures are supposed to protect us from. In other words, to "know the enemy." Only then will we be in a position to understand how these protective measures should work, which is the "know yourself" part of things.

Most of the protective measures I discuss in this book fall into the realm of *preventive security*. This means that rather than wait for the enemy to strike, we take the initiative and proactively prevent the hostile entity from reaching the execution phase of their attack. We don't wait around to target the attack itself, we target the hostile planning process that takes place *before* the attack comes. I go a bit deeper into this in Chapter 4, but generally, from the perspective of the hostile entity, the hostile planning process includes four phases: 1) collecting information on the target, 2) forming an action plan around the collected information, 3) executing the attack, and 4) if relevant, escaping and exploiting. Therefore, from the standpoint of prevention, the most vulnerable point in the hostile planning process is step 1—when the hostile entity goes out to collect information from the field and conducts hostile surveillance on the target.

Throughout the book, you'll find that it's this vulnerable step—the act of hostile surveillance—that most of the protective measures I'll be discussing are supposed to detect and/or disrupt. With that said, security professionals have numerous tactics and strategies at their disposal which they can use to deal with potential threats—including both conventional and unconventional means—so let's take a look.

CONVENTIONAL AND UNCONVENTIONAL PROTECTIVE OPERATIONS

What I define as *conventional protective operations* is basically anything that people can expect to find or can clearly see. A good example of this is your standard, uniformed officer or campus security guard force. It's your basic "what you see is what you get" type of deal.

On the other hand, *unconventional protective operations* are those that are either completely unseen or visually discreet. This means that most people will either not notice these protective measures, or not fully understand them. Both conventional and unconventional operations can (and often should) be employed at the same locations—oftentimes simultaneously. It's just a question of how things are performed, by whom, and for what purpose.

So let's take a moment to look at a couple of areas where conventional and unconventional operations can converge: executive protection and protective intelligence.

Executive Protection

When we get into the field of executive protection (EP), we find quite a few cases where the lines between conventional and unconventional operations become a bit blurry. The reason for this is because the main asset to be protected is a person rather than a building or property. Individuals (especially wealthy, important, and high-profile ones) tend to travel a lot or otherwise move around between different locations. To make matters even more complex, a large part of EP often covers the family of the individual in question, which can get tricky when you consider that protective coverage can be extended to the individual's residence, spouse, children, family trips, and more.

On the face of it, as long as the presence of the EP operators can be seen, I still consider it somewhat conventional. But as soon as protection starts taking on a low-profile characteristic, and definitely when it's done covertly, you get into the unconventional realm.

If you think that unconventional protective operations are full of action and intrigue, let me assure you that it's usually just the opposite. Despite having security concerns, many wealthy individuals (especially in the Silicon Valley) simply don't like the appearance of security all around them and their families. And in order to facilitate this, the unconventional approach is applied—quietly and without fanfare.

This isn't to say that there aren't some interesting and exciting situations out there—and I'm actually going to share a few of these stories with you—but it's important to point out that these short bursts of activity usually punctuate long stretches of tedium and boredom.

Protective Intelligence

Another slice of the conventional-unconventional dichotomy can be found in the field of protective intelligence—which is where I spend much of my time. Protective intelligence refers to *actionable information* that can be used for establishing and maintaining safety and security.

However, this intelligence doesn't necessarily have to be collected covertly or unconventionally. You can, for example, simply ask for information and make your intentions known. But there are some obvious trade-offs to this, and when pros and cons are weighed, the decision can also be made to collect intelligence more discreetly.

There are a number of ways to do this. Information can be collected remotely, on the cyber realm, through open sources (OSINT) and other, how shall I say it, not so open sources. But my specific field of expertise is when protective intelligence needs to include a covert field element. And it's these types of unconventional field intelligence operations that much of the book will concentrate on.

THE REALITIES OF PRIVATE SECURITY

Close your eyes and imagine what kind of physical security the top 50 corporations on the Fortune 500 list have, and what kind of protection their owners and top executives receive. Many people tend to assume that these individuals must live in a bubble of security, or otherwise lead some kind of high-tech, James Bond villain lifestyle. Hollywood has definitely done its part in perpetuating this notion. But the funny thing about this hype is that the reality (or at least everything I've seen in the last decade or more) would both disappoint you and completely blow your mind at the same time.

I use the term disappointing only in reference to Hollywood's glamorized depictions. In reality, it's actually kind of reassuring to discover that many of the most famous and influential people on the planet lead largely normal lives, in normal houses, with normal cars and offices. I know it may sound surprising for many people to hear that multi-billionaires—some of whom head the largest and most important Silicon Valley corporations—quite regularly drop their kids off at school (oftentimes in jeans and a T-shirt), get their coffee at Starbucks in the morning and go home to their families at the end of the day, just like everyone else.

And though there are those who do indeed enjoy basking in their fame and fortune, most executives I know prefer to simply be left alone to live a quiet and normal a life. I can also tell you that most of the CEOs I've worked for were extremely reluctant when it came to implementing security measures, and many resisted it as long as they could. In fact, later on in the book, I'll tell you of a case where I was hired to covertly protect a CEO who didn't even know that I and another covert operator were there.

I actually find the fact that many executives lead normal lives somewhat encouraging. I don't just mean in the silly sense of discovering that the rich and famous are "just like us," but in the sense that—despite everything you keep hearing in the media about the world being a crazy and dangerous place—most of the population, including some of the wealthiest and most influential people, can still generally lead normal, quiet lives.

On the other side of the ledger, there are also executives and organizations that employ levels of security that probably far exceed most people's imagination. To me, the irony has always been found in the contrasts that exist within a single corporation—or in the life of a single executive.

For example, some corporate facilities have areas where outsiders easily manage to tailgate or talk themselves into an office area right next to other areas with Mission Impossible-style security measures. Some of the tech moguls who often go unprotected to their children's school plays or to community center functions can, at other times, be surrounded by advanced security technology and covert protection that exceed most people's assumptions about what a James Bond villain would have. And if you too happen to find an irony or even a paradox in any of this, then let me officially welcome you to the world of high-end protective operations.

COMMON MISCONCEPTIONS

Any time you're dealing with covert or unconventional operations, people are going to come up with some pretty wild and imaginative ideas about it. So let me address a few of the common misconceptions that I've heard over the years.

First, I want to address the idea that there's something sinister about the high-level security that multinational corporations and billionaire executives receive. To a certain degree, I get it. With so many novels, movies, and TV shows out there spinning ominous tales, it isn't surprising that a lot of people start believing that corporate interests, wealthy individuals, and private sector security must, by definition, be up to no good. So let's get a few fundamentals out of the way:

1. **As private security professionals, we deal with security and protection for our clients and their companies.** Many people might think that the CEOs of major corporations and billionaire tech moguls are somehow impervious to threats as they sit in their well-secured fortresses. But I can tell you from experience that threats of physical harm (which are far from rare) affect them pretty much the same way they affect anyone else. Think whatever you want about the "lifestyles of the rich and famous," but these people have jobs, families, and kids, and they worry about them just like the rest of us. Those of us who work in private security are simply there to keep them safe.

2. **The security of our clients doesn't require putting anyone else at risk.** If anything, it's the other way around. The best way to protect our clients is to ensure that the entire area is safe and secure—for everyone. "But what about cases where someone wants to harm your client?," you might ask. Well, there too the best way to protect the client is either to avoid

the area altogether or to ensure that the area is safe and secure for everyone—including those who want to do harm. On numerous occasions, I've had to jump in between clients, or members of the organization I was protecting, and those who were trying to harm or otherwise harass them. Harming those who want to harm our clients is an absolute last resort—and an extremely rare one at that. In almost every case, the goal is to make sure that no one gets hurt on either side.

3. **The vast majority of the operators in this industry are honest, moral people.** Most of us are military veterans, former or current law enforcement officers, firefighters, paramedics, and former government agents. Working in dark suits or operating covertly doesn't suddenly make you less of a good, moral person. And though, like in every industry, we'll get the occasional bad apple, these individuals either get screened out during the hiring process or flush themselves out very quickly. Mean spirited or overly-aggressive individuals simply don't fit the high-level security environment.

Now that we've cleared much of the brush out of the way, covered some of the basics, and explained a bit about the industry, let me share some of my own story with you, and give you a better idea of where this book is coming from.

CHAPTER 2

WHO I AM

Before I get into the real meat of the book, I thought I'd take a little time to let you in on my background.

One of the strange and interesting things that happened to me while writing this book is that I realized how certain aspects of surveillance, surveillance detection and covert operations can be traced back to how I was raised and where my unconventional life has led me. For those of you who just want to get on with the main content of the book, feel free to skip over this chapter. But if you want to find out a bit more about me, and understand how someone like me wound up where I am, please read on.

EARLY DAYS

Let's start from the beginning: I was born and raised on a small kibbutz (a communal farm) on the northwest tip of Israel—just three miles south of the Lebanese border. Because my father had immigrated to Israel from the United States and my mother from Canada, I grew up speaking both Hebrew and English. I never thought much of this, since many of my friends had the exact same background and upbringing.

In retrospect, however, I think being bilingual played a significant part in getting me to where I am now. Language is much more than words and sentences; it represents a complete way of thinking and expressing yourself. Being bilingual doesn't just mean you can fluently speak two languages; it means you can *think* two different ways. I'm virtually a different person in Hebrew than I am in English, and the ability to slip in and out of different personalities is a skill I've made good use of over the years.

Another advantage of being bilingual, especially in such different languages as Hebrew and English, is that it made it easier to learn additional languages (and therefore think even more different ways). It took me quite a few years to realize I had a knack for languages because I wasn't a very good student in school. I was such a bad and rowdy student during seventh grade Arabic classes that my teacher actually hit me over the head with a heavy book and threatened to kill me. By the time I got to the eighth grade, I was officially kicked out of Arabic class, and to this day I'm embarrassed I don't speak the language.

It was only after graduating from high school that I discovered my affinity for learning new languages. This realization came in the form of a Swedish girlfriend who spent a few months on my kibbutz as part of the *Volunteer* working holiday program. Though her English was close to perfect, I wanted to impress her and her friends by throwing around a few words and sentences in Swedish. By asking questions and writing down sentences on pieces of scrap paper, I was carrying on simple conversations in Swedish after only a few weeks. It got to the point where it wasn't even about impressing my girlfriend anymore; I just really wanted to become as proficient as I could in

Swedish. In fact, I got even better at it after she went back to Sweden.

It was around that time (age 17–18) that I fell deeply in love with martial arts and started training and sparring with whomever I could find. I went through karate, kung-fu, Krav Maga, tae-kwon-do, ninjutsu and whatever techniques the ex-special forces guys I knew could teach me.

Slowly but surely, I came up with the dream of going to Japan to study Aikido. This dream was a pretty unlikely one as is, and no one I knew actually took me seriously. But standing in the way was an even bigger problem—a time-consuming and potentially dangerous one—mandatory military service in the Israeli Defense Forces (IDF).

IDF

For various reasons, I'm not going to give many details about my military service. It's impossible to summarize or adequately convey what an IDF service is like. I can tell you that during my service, I become a tank commander and then a staff sergeant, and got to experience quite a few things in quite a few places. My service took me from lush, green mountainous terrain to desolate, desert flatlands and from large, comfortable bases with amenities, swimming pools, and female instructors to small, dangerous outposts in Southern Lebanon, where we came under fire on a daily basis.

My military service was, for the most part, not all that bad by mid 1990s standards. That said, I came under fire enough times, escaped some really close calls and lost enough friends to make me truly grateful I got out in one piece. All those mortar rounds in Lebanon managed to miss me. All those anti-tank missiles were shot at tanks I wasn't in. All those machine gun bullets that accidentally hit my tank during training (as my head was sticking out of the tank) didn't hit me. The hand grenade that sprayed my tank with shrapnel only caught one of my fingers that was sticking out (I yanked out the piece of "frag" from my finger myself). And all those times I came really close to getting my head crushed or having a limb snapped off in the tank were somehow narrowly avoided. As I walked out of the discharge office in the end of my service, I ceremonially patted myself down to take inventory: two legs, two arms, two balls and a fully functional head on my shoulders. All in all, not too bad—too many people I knew didn't make it out as well as that.

Though pretty much everyone I knew had told me that by the time I got out of the army my Japan dream would have faded from memory, it only got stronger as time progressed. It took me about a year after the army to sort out all the details, finances, and various other issues, but in September of 1998 I finally landed in Tokyo.

The next stage of my life had begun.

JAPAN-US-CANADA-JAPAN

I had originally entered Japan on a tourist visa, which gave me three months to be in the country. I booked a three-month stay at the closest hostel I could find to my aikido dojo and put every ounce of my energy into training.

This was no ordinary dojo. In my mind, nothing but the best would do, so I went straight to the top—to the international headquarters of aikido—the founder's school—known as the Aikikai Hombu Dojo. I entered the dojo as a complete beginner, having never even set foot on an aikido mat before. As hard as it was, I insisted on taking every single beginner's class on the schedule, which amounted to three classes a day.

Sometime during my three-month stay, I began to understand I had a major problem on my hands. Before departing to Japan, I was in a serious relationship and even living with my then-girlfriend. We had desperately tried to square my martial arts dreams with our desire to be together, which was why I only went to Japan for three months. We had one of those classic tear-soaked airport goodbyes during which we kept reminding ourselves that it would only be for three months.

But now that I was finally living my childhood dream, could I just give it all up after three months and go back to Israel? It felt like torture—being pulled in two opposite directions. But half-way through my stay, my girlfriend decided to rid me of this dilemma and dumped me.

The experience was devastating. Not only was I dumped on the phone (standing in a dank Shinjuku public phone booth), but adding to my shattered heart was the fact that in my absence, I had been effectively evicted from our shared apartment. My now ex-girlfriend had packed up everything I owned and mailed it to my parents' house in cardboard boxes.

I had no home to go back to, and my visa was going to expire in a few weeks. I decided I would stay in Japan, but this meant I had to sort out my visa issue. The idea of going in and out of the country on tourist visas every three months didn't appeal to me, so I began to look for a long-term solution.

Having an American father and a Canadian mother means that in addition to my Israeli citizenship, I also have both American and Canadian citizenships. (I have three passports.) Searching for a good, long-term setup to extend my stay in Japan, I came across the Canadian Working Holiday Visa. There was just one problem—this visa could only be obtained from a Japanese embassy or consulate *in Canada*.

At that point, I already had to exit Japan before my tourist visa expired, so I accepted the offer of relatives to stay with them in Los Angeles until I sorted out my next steps. This took a bit longer than I expected, but eight weeks later, off to Canada I went (in February, of all times).

It's a curious thing to enter a country you've never been to before as a full citizen. It almost felt like cheating, the way the Canadian customs officer barely glanced at my unused Canadian passport, and welcomed me "back home" without even stamping the thing.

In Canada, things proved to be trickier than I had expected.

Working my way through the long visa application process necessitated, how shall I say, a bit of creativity. The Canadian-Japanese Working Holiday Visa is available only to Canadian residents, and the application forms included having to detail where I lived and worked in Canada, where I grew up in Canada, and even which Canadian high school I graduated from. And all this was to be followed by an in-person interview at the Japanese consulate.

In retrospect, this was one of the turning points of my life. I could either back down from the idea, which meant I would probably have to go back to Israel (to stay at my parents' house), or I could invent a new Canadian identity for myself and keep going. I decided on the latter.

In order to pull this off, I would need to create an elaborate cover story. Not only did I have to put the invented details of my Canadian life on paper, I had to also commit them to memory for my interview at the consulate. What I discovered (and have subsequently made good use of professionally) is that a good cover story shouldn't include any interesting details. If you just make it boring enough, no one is tempted to dig too deeply into it.

My identity was of a 23-year-old Canadian from Waterloo, Ontario—a boring town about an hour south of Toronto, and where I was actually staying. My mother was from Montreal (which was true), and I was born in Israel (a fact I couldn't cover up, since it appeared on my passport). The rest of my Canadian identity was completely invented however. I was basically unemployed since graduating from some unimportant high school in Waterloo and had never been to Japan before (this only appeared on my American passport). All my papers were in order, and the Japanese interviewer at the consulate practically yawned himself through my interview.

A few weeks later I was on a flight from Toronto to Tokyo—Working Holiday Visa in hand. I had left Israel as an Israeli, entered Japan and the U.S. as an American, and after a few weeks in Ontario, was on my way back to Japan as a Canadian.

AIKIDO

Aikido falls in the category of "soft" martial arts. This means that rather than using "hard" strikes and blocks, aikido techniques redirect the opponent's energy and use it against him. Many people can't quite see beyond aikido's joint manipulations and flashy throws, but aikido takes you very deeply into the mechanics, psychology, and even spirituality of body mechanics, power, movement and flow. The key to most aikido techniques is to find various unconventional, oftentimes surprising ways to redirect and unbalance your opponent. Once this is achieved, you can throw him, lock him up, or subdue him.

Though I had, by the time I arrived in Japan, established a solid, hard martial arts basis, I always thought that aikido more suited my flexible and unconventional mindset. This proved to be very much the case, and aikido further deepened my flexibility and adaptability.

After returning to Japan, I again threw myself hard and deep into my martial arts training, and even added an ancient stick-fighting art to my aikido studies. As committed as I had been to martial arts up until that point, this is when I became an outright fanatic.

As overdramatic as it sounds now, at the time it felt like I lost everything I had in pursuit of my dream. Martial arts training not only became the only thing I wanted to do; it felt like the only thing that gave my life any meaning.

It might sound like a pretty dark place to be in, but there's something intoxicating, even addictive, about living a completely pure and focused life—one with no nuances, confusions or strings attached. Though I later became weary of most types of fanaticism, having personally experienced a very potent form of it, I definitely understand its romantic allure. It makes me laugh a bit to recall this, but I remember feeling like I was starring in my own action-adventure movie. I was the hero who had lost everything, and was now on some desperate do-or-die martial arts quest in a faraway land.

I do believe there are many benefits to pushing yourself beyond your natural limits, as I did at the time, but in retrospect, I can't endorse the unhealthy level to which my fanaticism took me. Every ache or injury I sustained on the training mat was met by nothing less than my pounding it out till it relented and went away. It got to a point where my right shoulder would sometimes dislocate on the mat, and I would pop it back in myself, then continue training after a short break.

Nevertheless, maintaining this level of intensity not only earned me two first degree black belts after only two years, it completely altered the way I walk, move and think. Far beyond mere physicality, aikido is an entire philosophy—teaching you how to flow, adapt, and surreptitiously unbalance and undermine opponents. It teaches you a great deal about yourself and about other people, and I have subsequently made good use of the habits it has instilled in me.

LEARNING JAPANESE

Another undertaking I invested myself in was learning the Japanese language. I had neither the time nor the money for any formal education, so I applied my previously discovered penchant for languages to learning Japanese. To pull this off, I bought a few textbooks and dictionaries and sought out any opportunity to practice words and phrases with the people around me. Within about three months, I was able to carry out simple (and even some not so simple) conversations. And within six months, I was freaking out a few of my friends with my conversation abilities.

The beauty of learning a new language is that it's so much more than just acquiring a mechanism for communication. It quite literally introduces you to a whole new world. I already knew a bit of this, having grown up bilingual and picking up Swedish, but that didn't come close to what I experienced when I learned Japanese.

After you spend a bit of time in a foreign country, let alone a country as unique as Japan, you get used to being surrounded by the sounds of an alien culture and people (in point of fact, it's actually *you* who is the alien). But when you learn the language (especially as quickly as I did), the notion of "far-away exotic land" gets quickly replaced with familiarity and even a strange sense of belonging. I would catch myself, say, eating lunch at a ramen shop or sitting on a train, and realize I understood everyone's conversations around me. It seemed like five minutes earlier I had been surrounded by "strange sounds in an exotic Asian locale", now it was just people talking about their work, a kid asking his mom for a treat, a young woman asking her boyfriend to call her when he got back from his weekend trip, and so on.

Lest you think I'm complaining about my "exotic Asian wonderland" being suddenly replaced by normal mundane life, let me assure you—It was just the opposite. I can't tell you how exciting it was (albeit in a different way) to suddenly understand people. It so brilliantly reaffirmed the fact that we're all the same, that everyone in the world is essentially dealing with the same kind of stuff. Of course, any thinking person already knows this on one level or another, but it really does make a difference when you experience it in such an intense way. To me, this is when I stopped being a tourist and firmly became a resident of Japan. And this is why to this day, Japan still feels like home to me.

I had somewhat of a similar experience when I taught myself to read and write. The Japanese language has three different writing systems that are blended together: Kanji (漢字) are Chinese characters, or ideograms (numbering in the thousands). Hiragana (ひらがな) and Katakana (カタカナ) are two simpler systems of phonetic letters.

My learning process started with my closing myself off in my tiny room for an entire weekend of cramming both Hiragana and Katakana into my head. Learning so quickly how to read a new language (or at least a small portion of it) once again had quite a freaky effect. I remember emerging from my tiny room on Monday morning to go to aikido practice, walking down the same familiar streets on the way to the dojo, and suddenly being able to read many of the familiar signs I had gotten used to seeing. All those exotic, cryptic Asian symbols suddenly just told me things like "ramen shop," "laundromat" and "fruit store" (where, by the way, "apples are on sale").

CREATING A FALSE IDENTITY

Learning how to create false identities and cover stories is something people usually associate with trainees who've been recruited into intelligence agencies. My own self-taught introduction to this field wasn't nearly as important or dramatic as that, but it was certainly extensive. It began when I had to convince the Japanese consulate in Toronto that I was a born and bred Canadian, but it really reached its peak when I had to invent yet another identity in Tokyo, and maintain it for years.

Finding work in Tokyo was a real challenge for me when I first started out. Most English speakers simply went for the job of English language teacher. So I started answering job ads, and was invited to a few interviews. It became very apparent however that I had a big problem. The demand in the adult learning market was primarily for Americans who could give their pupils a fun experience of learning from, and conversing with, an all-American guy. I, on the other hand, was an Israeli (just out of the IDF) who also had American citizenship but who was living in Japan on a Canadian visa. Pretty much everyone who interviewed me thought that was "very interesting," but I would get no job offer in the end.

Since I was seriously running out of money at that stage, I realized that I had to take a different approach. It once again hit me that I didn't really have anywhere to go back to, and that I had lost everything just to be where I was. I had left Japan to go all the way to Canada via the U.S. to get a work visa. I was finally living my martial arts dream, and now it was all about to go down the toilet because I couldn't get a fucking job to afford staying there. It was just too much to take. If an all-American guy was what people wanted, and if that was the only thing that could keep me in Japan, then by god that's what I'd give 'em.

The person I invented for this role was Michael Toben, an LA native whose mother was from Canada (hence the visa), and who could—and did—talk at length about what life was like in LA, what he liked doing there for fun, and even, if necessary, which LA high school he had graduated from (John Marshall High School).

I based much of this identity on my father's (who was born and raised in Los Angeles) and on what I knew, having spent a good amount of time there myself. People loved it. By the end of that year I was teaching at two vocational schools and one after-school children's center and had lots of private lessons I was teaching all around town. It got to where I had to turn down offers because work was taking over too much training time.

Many people who achieve a level of expertise in a certain field only get to that level because they have no other choice. In my case, I would either become an expert at maintaining a false identity or go hungry and be forced to leave everything I had worked so hard to achieve. I opted for the former and got so good at maintaining my false identity that it became a natural part of me. Michael Toben had an entire professional and social life that comprised dozens of people who employed me, worked with me, took my classes, befriended me, went out with me, and even invited me to their homes to meet their families.

Maintaining a false identity for such a long period of time tends to produce some, how shall I put it, "interesting" situations—especially when multiple people in the same city knew either one identity or the other (or, in some cases, both). Talking on the phone was sometimes a challenge. I would by default answer the phone in English, and in some situations (when I was with someone who knew me as Michael) would have to continue talking in English even though the person on the other end of the line was an Israeli friend talking to me in Hebrew. (My Israeli friends knew what was going on and would often tease me about it.)

One place where this "situation" came to a head was my favorite bar in the Shinjuku district. I spent a good amount of time there with my Israeli friends who were living in town and became quite friendly with the bartender. One evening, one of my longtime students wanted to take me out for drinks after her private lesson. She insisted on taking me to one of her favorite bars in Shinjuku, which, as you can already guess, turned out to be the same bar I frequented. She, it turned out, had also become friendly with the bartender, and after insisting on our sitting at the bar, promptly introduced me to him as Michael. Most good bartenders (especially Japanese ones) adhere to the unwritten code of discretion that their profession entails. But I was both grateful for, and impressed by, how naturally he played along and pretended to meet "Michael" for the first time. The next time I went there for a drink (carefully checking to see that my client wasn't there), I thanked him for his impeccable performance, and we both had a good laugh about it.

It was only a decade later, when I was getting into the surveillance detection field, that I realized how useful my Tokyo experience had become. In fact, there have been undercover situations in Israel and in the United States when I brought Michael Toben out of retirement. I still do it from time to time, and it feels good to slip back into his familiar identity. It's like putting on an old favorite jacket you keep in your closet, or reliving some nostalgic memory.

COMING TO AMERICA

During my fourth year in Japan, I was beginning to realize that as much as I loved it there, I was outgrowing my small life of training and teaching English. Having met many Americans in Tokyo over the years, it became apparent to me that an American university degree tended to swing academic and professional doors wide open, and seemed to be a common denominator of a larger, more interesting life in Japan. It didn't even seem to matter what the degree was in as long as it was from a reputable university. Many of my acquaintances had degrees in Asian Studies or Japanese, which suited me just fine.

The fact that I had barely managed to graduate from high school in Israel didn't deter me (not after all I'd been through), and I came up with a plan to temporarily move to the U.S., go to a top university, and then return to Japan—diploma in hand—ready to advance myself to the next level.

The first part of the plan worked quite well. I wanted to stay on the West Coast of the United States (in order to be closer to Japan) and find a reputable university in a city that also had a well-connected aikido dojo. I found this exact combination in Berkeley, California. Upon my arrival, I quickly joined the Berkeley Aikikai dojo (which is owned by the famous Ichiro Shibata sensei) and enrolled in a junior college in order to acquire enough credits to transfer to the University of California, Berkeley. It took a bit longer than I originally planned, but I eventually managed to achieve my goal—graduating from UC Berkeley with a degree in Japanese language and literature.

The second part of the plan—the one that had me returning to Japan with my diploma—didn't quite work out. But this seemingly disappointing outcome is responsible for the most important things in my life now: the family I have in San Francisco, my professional career, and this very book you're reading right now.

MY LIFE IN SECURITY

By 2004, I'd been living in California for a couple of years and found my interests in politics (especially Middle Eastern politics) reigniting. I had been almost completely oblivious to any and all political affairs during my time in Japan. But living in Berkeley gave me a front-row seat from which to observe the upheaval surrounding the Iraq war and the ultra-violent second intifada (uprising) that was raging in Israel and the Palestinian territories.

An Israeli friend of mine had told me when I first arrived that living in Berkeley would test my left wing, liberal leanings (which I got from my upbringing), and he was correct. What I experienced during those early years in the Bay Area would forever change my political views.

I would see banners and stickers with the Star of David being equated to a swastika. I would encounter blood-dripping Israeli flags and anti-Semitic caricatures (featuring fanged, big-nosed, murderous Jews). I would have people tell me—to my face—that my family in Israel should "Go back to Poland," and that if they didn't, they deserved to be blown to shreds by Palestinian suicide bombers.

Though I wasn't living in the Middle East at the time, the San Francisco Bay Area was the perfect place to see how the leftist anti-war and anti-Israel movements (which had been largely nonviolent) were being co-opted by local, and even some international, elements with extremist agendas. Much of this would later be dubbed the *"Regressive Left,"* and watching its formation was truly alarming.

I would see well-meaning but empty-headed members of organizations like *Code Pink* and *Jewish Voice For Peace* standing right next to young Islamists in ski masks and Kafiya face covers, yelling and chanting profanities in Arabic. Though I don't consider myself an Arabic speaker, my Arabic was good enough to understand their shouts to "kill the Jews" and the chants that "Jews are our dogs," which the monolingual hippies and hipsters who were standing next to them (many of whom were Jewish themselves) were too ignorant to understand.

It's a bizarre thing to see liberals and pacifists protest in favor of ruthless dictatorships (like that of Saddam Hussein) and support violent theocratic organizations (like Hamas, Islamic Jihad and Hezbollah). I still had very vivid memories of running into our safe-room and putting on my gas mask as Saddam Hussein's missiles were exploding in Israel back during the first Gulf War. I had friends and family members who very narrowly avoided being killed by the suicide bombers of Hamas and Islamic Jihad. And I had lived most of my life being shot at by the Hezbollah organization, which was lobbing rockets into my kibbutz, and which had killed army friends of mine in Lebanon. Experiencing all of this, along with my increasing interest in intelligence and counter-terrorism, is what ultimately led me to the high-end security industry. I was tired of seeing what was going on from my front-row seat and decided to trade it in for a frontline position.

As an Israeli with military experience, getting into the security industry wasn't much of a stretch, and I was proud to start working for an Israeli-run company that provided high-end terrorist activity prevention services to Jewish and Israeli clients. While my security work also served as a convenient college job, my dedication to it was quickly noticed, and before long, I was rising up in the ranks of what turned out to be a rapidly growing security company. By 2008, I had acquired quite a bit of field experience and had worked for or alongside many political organizations, Fortune 500 corporations, the Israeli government, wealthy Silicon Valley executives, Jewish organizations, multiple foreign governments, and every single law enforcement and federal agency in the San Francisco Bay Area.

Four years of work experience at this level caused me to believe that I had a solid grasp on high-end protective services. I had developed a highly effective hostile activity prevention program and had helped take the company's field operations, training, and supervision departments to a higher level. But all of this was about to change when in the summer of 2008, I was sent to Israel to receive surveillance detection training.

DOWN THE RABBIT HOLE OF SURVEILLANCE DETECTION

Having never formally trained in surveillance detection before, I wrongly assumed that the course I was entering would largely cover the type of work I had spent four years becoming proficient at. I therefore expected my skills in terrorist activity prevention to help me succeed in the course and entered it with quite a bit of confidence. As it turned out, nothing could have knocked that false sense of confidence out of me faster than the Israeli surveillance detection course I took.

For me, the most earth-shattering thing about that course was how it undermined my notion of reality. I could say that it changed the way I would forever look at the field of security, but that would be a gross understatement. The course taught me how to look at everything and everyone in a completely different way, and I couldn't turn it off—even when I wanted to. I tried hard to go back to the comfortable ignorance I had been living in, but it was almost impossible to ignore what I now knew. Like getting yanked out of the Matrix, once your eyes are opened, there's really no going back.

To summarize what the course taught me, it began with how to conduct hostile surveillance, gain crucial information, and penetrate secured locations on a level that would be invisible even to experienced security professionals. It then went to an even deeper level, teaching me how to detect such surveillance activities and how to do so without the covert surveillant knowing about it.

The course was almost exclusively conducted in the field and ranged (quite wildly) from the Tel-Aviv beachfront to the ancient, bustling markets of Jerusalem's Old City. Incorporated into the field exercises were trainers and hostile surveillance role-players who had real-world government sector experience in these types of things. There was nothing theoretical about it, and my trainers were introducing me to a hidden yet very real dimension of life that existed all around me (and everyone else for that matter).

I would have loved to boast about how I used my earlier training and experience to detect these individuals, but the little that I did manage (right at the end) was pretty much due to their purposely allowing me to detect them so I could experience at least a modicum of success. To say that this was a humbling experience would be yet another understatement.

It turned out that in addition to my inability to detect the hostile surveillance activities they were role-playing for me, these experienced professionals had also been covertly following and keeping tabs on me pretty much the entire time I was out in the field. I was even shown photographic proof of this. When I met some of them after my final exercise, they gave me a rundown of what I needed to improve on. The list was quite long. They were nice enough to put a positive and even encouraging face on it, but the fact of the matter was that it really cut me down to size. It was by far the most humbling experience I've had in my professional career, but it subsequently propelled me to a much higher level.

After returning to the U.S., I realized that the lasting effects of this course were going to be a challenge. It hit me that what had previously seemed like well-secured facilities now looked completely naked and vulnerable. Telling my boss as much (and wording it far more strongly than I should have) made him understandably upset with me. After all, it was he who had sent me to this course so I could bring back the knowledge of how to enhance our protective capabilities. And now here I was telling him that it was pointless, that we would need to turn the entire company upside down to even get close. Every security professional now seemed clueless and vulnerable, and I contemplated leaving the company, and the industry, altogether. It just seemed pointless.

It took me a little while to realize that as much as I had learned about the world, I would also need to learn how to balance it out—or more exactly, balance myself out. To a certain extent, every place is vulnerable to people with the set of skills I had learned—especially to those who are way more skilled and experienced than me. But there's not much use in dwelling in fear.

In the years since I've taken the course, my skills have largely improved precisely *because* I learned how to calm down and relax during field operations. No one goes through life without accepting a certain amount of risk. Those of us who work in high-level security aren't any different—we just know much more about the risks and therefore have much more to accept.

I'm going to end this little autobiography here since much of what I've been up to since my surveillance detection training will be revealed throughout the book. The purpose of this chapter was to give you a glimpse into my unconventional life, and to explain how I ended up where I am today.

Now, let's get things going.

In the following chapters, I'll let you in on the secrets of the trade, tell you some true stories from the field, and reveal the largely unknown world of surveillance, surveillance detection and unconventional protective operations.

CHAPTER 3

INDUCTIVE OBSERVATION: WATCHING & UNDERSTANDING PEOPLE

> *"The ideal reasoner," he remarked, "Would, when he had once been shown a single fact in all its bearings, deduce from it not only all the chain of events which led up to it but also all the results which would follow from it."*
>
> —Arthur Conan Doyle,
> The Adventures of Sherlock Holmes

One of the things that makes security and field intelligence so interesting is that they're mostly about people. Protective efforts, even if assisted by security systems, are usually directed *at* people and largely executed *by* people for the protection *of* people. The most important assets are usually people, most of the highest risks we try to mitigate have to do with people, and most surveillance detection, screening, and assessment efforts are attempts to distinguish between people who pose a security risk and those who do not.

If you can't understand people, you can't fully understand how to assess and mitigate security risks.

LEARNING TO READ PEOPLE

Back when I was living in Tokyo, I met a fellow Israeli named Danny who became my closest friend during my years in Japan. Before even reaching adulthood, Danny had become quite a successful entrepreneur. He was also very much in love with Asian art and culture, and this is what eventually brought him to Tokyo, where he had been living for a decade before I arrived. A self-educated, self-made millionaire, Danny was a natural businessman, world traveler, art history expert, connoisseur of fine foods and high-end spirits, and fluent speaker of five or six languages. A fascinating jet-setter–Indiana Jones combination, he was and still is a real-life "Most Interesting Man in the World."

Of the many things that Danny taught me, the most lasting and useful one was the art of people—how to read them, how to understand true intentions hiding behind nuanced expressions, how to read conscious and subconscious mannerisms, and how to use this type of knowledge to gain various advantages.

This type of outward focus has to start with inward self-reflection. In other words, part of understanding other people is understanding and controlling your *own* weaknesses, body language, nuanced expressions, and emotional states. We would go out and practice our people-reading and people-influencing skills, mostly in the arenas of Tokyo's upscale neighborhoods—with their snazzy cafés, restaurants, and clubs. It was like a wide-open game of chess where you'd carefully position yourself and try to calculate a few steps ahead as you played along. We would then evaluate how things went, discussing what worked and what didn't.

During my first visit back to Israel, after being away for over a year, the full effect of what I had learned in Japan started to hit me. People might be people no matter where they live, but culture *does* matter when it comes to how people express themselves. When it comes to Japanese culture, especially in high-end circles, people are very reserved and desires are conveyed very subtly, camouflaged behind layers of politeness.

Israelis, by contrast (and Americans, in a different way) are somewhere on the opposite end of this spectrum. Having toiled for months getting used to reading the subtleties of Japanese behavior made me feel almost clairvoyant when I arrived in Israel. People seemed so childishly obvious, even when they were trying not to be. Everyone's emotional states, desires, motivations, and actions were just splayed out in plain sight. It felt voyeuristic just to look at someone. Little did I know at the time that this developed skill would become very useful in my professional future.

Being able to read people—to deduce and induce various things about them—is extremely useful for protective and field intelligence operations. So let me give you a crash-course and share some secrets of the trade.

WHAT TO LOOK FOR

One of the things that never really sat right with me as a young security operator (and that I try to avoid repeating as a trainer today) was being told that, when it comes to reading people, you should "Trust your instincts." Don't get me wrong, it's not a mistake to trust your instincts, but not everyone's instincts are that sharply developed, and even among those with better instincts, there's always room for improvement.

In many cases, "Trust your instincts" is not much more than a cop-out line to avoid having to explain *how* you can develop observation and assessment skills. Yes, always trust your instincts, but don't stop there. There's nothing magical or untouchable about instincts—they're perceptions that are caused by a blend of intakes you sense on a subliminal level. It's just that you're more conscious of the *perception* than you are of its subliminal *causes*, which is why an instinct feels more like a cause than an effect. But rather than treat instincts as some magical sixth sense, you can actually get to the bottom of what's causing them. By bringing these subtle sensory intakes out of their subliminal realm, you can sharpen your detection skills and develop even better instincts.

For example, did you see someone who looks completely normal and non-suspicious? Good, ask yourself what exactly about that person gave you that feeling. Did you see someone who struck you as oddly suspicious? Good, now ask yourself the same question. Look for the underlying reasons behind those instincts because they're there. Start raising your consciousness to *how* and *why* people look and behave the way they do. Try to detect, assess, and understand as many details as you can, and try to figure out the "why" factor *behind* those feelings you get about people. You're not always going to get it right, but with practice, you'll definitely get better and faster at it.

Appearance

When it comes to gauging appearance, the factors we want to evaluate and profile are the ones people have *chosen*. The idea of profiling often gets a bad rap, but this is usually caused by profiling being applied to factors that were *not* chosen, like race, age, and gender. The problem with racial profiling, for example, isn't only an ethical one, it's a logical one. It attempts to extrapolate conclusions about intent based on unchosen, unintentional features a person has no control over. This type of profiling is not only problematic when it leads to false-positive assumptions (usually against younger males and minority groups) but also—or especially—when it leads to false-negative assumptions (which can be very dangerous).

Luckily, the majority of what comprises a person's appearance *is* chosen—from their hair down to their shoes, and anything else they might be wearing, carrying, applying, or growing. Whoever coined the phrase "You can't judge a book by its cover" must have been talking about books because there's a hell of a lot we can tell about people if we pay attention to the details, and analyze them correctly. Nothing a person has on them is there randomly. What a person has chosen to wear, carry, or apply can tell you two important things in regards to the situation at hand:

1. **Where the person is coming from**—their background, tastes, and resources. What kind of person owns, say, tactical boots? What kind of person carries an expensive Gucci handbag? Why would a person be carrying a large gym bag? There are reasons for these things, and they all have to do with prior choices.

2. **Where the person is going**—why did they choose to wear, carry, or apply the thing you just noticed before coming to this place at this time? What might that mean about their motivations? What, for instance, might be the difference in motivation between a person wearing military-style boots and a person wearing flip-flops? What might be the future intent of the person wearing the quintessential heavy jacket on a warm day? It's interesting to think where the person carrying the gym bag is coming from, but what's even more important is why they're now trying to bring it with them to this place at this time. What might their intentions for the future be?

Are there any guarantees you'll be able to figure out people's backgrounds and future intentions based solely on their chosen appearance? Of course not, and many suspicious-looking indicators turn out to be perfectly harmless (if somewhat weird). But the more you notice, the more you'll think about what you're seeing. And the more questions you ask about things, the better your chances of figuring things out. This might sound like a drawn out narrative, but, with a bit of practice, most people can notice, think, ask, and conclude very quickly—almost as if it were, well, instinct.

By the way, the gym bag scenario might sound ominous—as in the possibility that a person might be trying to conceal a weapon or explosives. But more often than not there's a perfectly non-hostile reason behind it. I've noticed that in high-threat evening events in San Francisco, you're almost always going to encounter at least one person with a large gym bag (even if it's a dressy event). The bag obviously gets checked very well—which also means the person gets checked and questioned—but it almost always turns out that the person is simply coming from (surprise, surprise) the gym. People in San Francisco like going to the gym after work, and then, when they go to evening events, don't want to leave their bag in the car (if they even own a car). It's a perfectly harmless reason (except for the fact that I have to go through their sweaty gym bag...), but a *chosen* reason nonetheless; one that can tell you *where* the person is coming from and *why* they brought the thing in question to this place at this time. Just because something is harmless doesn't mean your observational skills and choice profiling don't apply.

An important side note to appearance in cases where you're close enough to the person in question, is scent. Now this might sound funny, or even a bit creepy, but what might you be able to induce about people with gym bags if they smell a bit sweaty? What can you assume if a person's hair is a bit wet and they smell of soap or shampoo? Try not to be overtly weird about this, but notice how people smell when they go to work in the morning and how they smell after they've had a long day. Who's got poor hygiene, who's been drinking or smoking, and who's using too much aftershave or perfume (possibly to mask some other odor)? Smell is one of the sensory intakes that often sits on a subliminal level. Bring it out of there and start consciously noticing it. The idea that something just doesn't smell right is oftentimes quite literal. The more you notice, the better your chances of detecting where people are coming from and what kind of choices they made before arriving.

Body language

Behavioral profiling is a pretty deep subject, but for our purposes, we're not necessarily looking for micro-expressions or psychological evaluations. Instead, we're interested in the *context* of the situation—where we are, what's going on, and how people are behaving in relation to these factors.

First of all, you won't be in a very good position to evaluate body language until you are somewhat acquainted with the way people ordinarily behave. Every environment is different in this regard, and even times of day make a difference, so it's important to establish a baseline for what "normal" or non-hostile behavior might look like. This isn't always that clear-cut, and you're going to have to accept a pretty wide range of behaviors. But keep in mind that 99.999% of the people you see are non-hostile and can therefore provide you with that baseline.

Remember, we're not just looking at people in general; we're looking at how people behave at a specific place, time, and context—especially if there's security presence in the area. How are people acting? Do their behaviors fall in line with those of most people at this place and time? Did one person nervously show up alone while most people seem cheerful as they show up in couples or groups? Were there people who showed up together and then split up? What might be the reasons for their behaving like that? Ask these questions because the reasons are always there.

In situations where access to a certain area is regulated, most people simply walk right up as if security isn't really a deterring factor to them because, guess what, it isn't. A non-hostile individual is probably thinking about why they're going to the secured location, rather than about having to *go through a security check*. And this will show in how they conduct themselves.

People with hostile intent usually exhibit different kinds of behavior. Exactly what kind of behavior indicates a person has hostile intent, or is otherwise trying to hide something, is a bit tricky to pin down since different people exhibit different behavioral patterns. For example, you might see a person walking quickly, "tunnel-visioned" on their target as they head straight towards it. Conversely, it's not uncommon to see people walking very slowly, looking around nervously, while stopping and starting their movement towards their target.

The fact that nervousness and hostile intent can manifest themselves in different ways might seem a bit confusing, but remember you're not looking for a positive psychological profile here. All you need to determine is that something in the person's behavior is abnormal—that it's different from the non-hostile baseline you've established. Be it too fast or too slow, tunnel-visioned, head on a swivel, or what have you, as soon as you realize this isn't the way most people move and behave in this environment, you've spotted something that needs a bit more attention.

As complex and varied as human behavior might be, there are a number of traits that are quite universal. People under stress will almost always have higher levels of adrenalin in their bloodstream, which produces some predictable results.

Adrenalin raises a person's blood pressure, which tends to make people hot and sometimes sweaty. Some people might get red in the face and ears, while others might become pale—either case can be bad news. High blood pressure makes people breathe faster, which dries up their mouths, causing them to swallow saliva awkwardly and generally making it harder for them to speak clearly. Try to notice if they keep shifting their weight uncomfortably and notice what they're doing with their hands. Are they fidgeting their fingers, white-knuckling, or clasping? What about their eyes? Are they completely avoiding eye contact or overcompensating by maintaining too much of it? Once again, as soon as you realize something doesn't quite fall in line with how most people behave in this situation, you've spotted something that needs a bit more attention.

PRACTICING OBSERVATION

One of the neat things about developing your observational skills is that you can practice observation and assessment anywhere and anytime—on the street, in a coffee shop, on the train, or during a ballgame. You can even do it right now if you want. Stop reading for a moment and look at what's on you. What kind of shoes are you wearing? (Shoes, from my experience, can tell you quite a bit about a person.) Do you have a wedding ring on your finger? Is your cell phone tucked in a pocket or purse, or is it somewhere else right now? What do your hands and fingernails look like, and why? What kind of clothes are you wearing at the moment, and what kind of watch, cell phone cover, or glasses do you have?

All of these things, and many more, result from choices you made *before* arriving to wherever you are right now. Even if you didn't give it much conscious thought at the time, these prior choices reflect certain things about you. And even if you received some items as gifts, your decision to have them on you in this place and at this time says something about you. It's basically a Sherlock Holmes-type game of observation and inductive reasoning—or what I like to call "inductive observation." The more you play it, the faster and better you'll get at it.

Keep pushing and testing yourself to see how quickly you can detect things, how many details you can detect in as short a time as possible, and whether your assessments about people's backgrounds and motivations were correct. Try playing the inductive observation game in situations where you actually get to talk to the individuals you've observed so you can find out if your hypotheses about them were correct. However, I recommend keeping this observational game to yourself during most social or professional settings since some people can get a bit creeped out by it.

Slowly but surely, you'll get better, faster, and more subtle at it. If your assessment about a person ends up being *correct*, good—file it in your memory and try to see if it also applies to other people in other situations. If your assessment was *incorrect*, that's also good—it means you're trying things out and learning. Keep going.

Finally, never forget to use your inductive observation skills on yourself before applying them to anyone else. Be conscious of your own appearance and body language, and knowingly utilize these to outwardly project an image that's appropriate for your situation. This is your chance to make an impression and shape what you want people to think about you, so use it wisely.

Everything about people's appearance and body language—everything they have on them, everything they do, everywhere they've been, and anywhere they're going—can tell you something about them. And the same principle applies to you as well.

In the coming chapters, as we delve deeper into surveillance, surveillance detection, and special protective operations, I'm going to show you how these factors can help you detect the intentions of others—particularly those with hostile intent—while masking your own intentions from them.

CHAPTER 4

HOSTILE SURVEILLANCE

San Francisco, 2009. South of Market district. My target was a large Silicon Valley startup. I had started my hostile planning process with an internet search on the company's headquarters and its surrounding area. The first item of interest for me was the fact that the company's headquarters were located in a shared office building.

There were at least two other companies in the same building and enough vacant office spaces for the property owners to advertise the availability of office space for rent. These factors would make it easier to enter the building and provided good material for a solid cover and cover story. Next, I noticed that there was a supermarket and a café across the street from the office building. This was also good news since it provided a good external vantage point from which to observe the office building.

Armed with this information, I went to the café (which was

attached to the supermarket), got a cup of coffee and a croissant, and sat down at a table with my laptop. I had a good view of my target through the coffee shop's large window, and not only could I see its main entrance, but I also had a clear line of sight on the very accessible loading dock. It was also nice to see how many of the company's workers were coming into the café and how easy it would be to strike up a casual conversation with them about their workplace. (I knew they were employees because they were wearing the typical logoed T-shirts and hoodies that Silicon Valley companies like to give their employees.) I could also see that security procedures were pretty lax and that the security guards were basically only there to keep homeless people from wandering in.

My next course of action was to see if I could get myself into the building and find out if I could get access to any key locations. If necessary, I would use the cover story that I'm looking for office space to rent and that the realtor (I had her actual name on hand in case the need arose) told me I could check out the property on my own. If this didn't work, my backup plan was to get in touch with her and actually schedule a walkthrough. The need for this did not arise, though.

Dressed in impeccably boring business-casual, holding my laptop, and maintaining a slight air of arrogance as I pretended to talk on my phone not only got me into the building, but gave me free range inside it, too. I strolled through office spaces, took a little rest in the cafeteria, and before long I was standing right outside the C-Suites, where the founder and CEO of the company was seated.

UNDERSTANDING HOSTILE SURVEILLANCE

At this point, you might be thinking that I was engaged in hostile surveillance. But to clarify, no, I wasn't actually after the CEO, and no, I wasn't actually trying to harm the company—quite the contrary. They were in fact the ones who had hired me. My assignment was to conduct a risk assessment on their headquarters and to find out how easy it would be for a potential hostile person to get access to their CEO.

The abovementioned operation is what's known as a Red-Team exercise or Penetration Test. These exercises are meant to find and expose security weaknesses by mimicking the actions of hostile surveillants. By doing this, you gain a more objective perspective on the target's vulnerabilities. And it's with this in mind that I want to delve into the subject of hostile surveillance.

While the term *surveillance* can be applied to various types of activities and electronic measures, what I'm referring to here is *human intelligence* (often abbreviated as HUMINT). This type of physical surveillance can be defined as *the covert observation of a target for the purpose of collecting information*. This short definition contains the three key ingredients of surveillance.

The first two ingredients are *covertness* and *physical observation*—take one of these factors out and you no longer have what we consider surveillance. If physical observation is done overtly, willingly allowing the target (or anyone else) to see it, then this would simply be physical observation rather than surveillance. Conversely, if an operative is conducting themselves in such a covert manner that they cannot really observe the target, then this would be a form of hiding rather than conducting surveillance.

The third ingredient of surveillance is *information collection*. After all, such challenging and risky activities aren't simply performed for the fun of it. The goal of hostile surveillance—the entire reason for doing it in the first place—is to collect crucial information that's necessary for planning an attack.

The first thing to understand about high-level surveillance is that it's a process that begins before any direct observation on the target takes place. You start out by gaining a better understanding of the area around the target first. Most importantly, the operative needs to locate at least one good vantage point on the target.

A *vantage point* is a location from which the operative can conduct surveillance, and a good surveillance vantage point is one that will give the operative access to important visual information while allowing them to collect this information covertly (combining covertness and observation). The best way to maintain covertness is for the surveillance operative to make it seem like they're doing something else—something harmless, boring, and unrelated to the target. The abovementioned café is one of my favorite types of vantage points because they make it easy to spend a lot of time there without arousing any suspicion.

Considering the amount of time that needs to be spent at a vantage point, it would be unwise for an operative to hastily position themself at that location before it has been better understood. This is because if the operative is not in tune with the appearance and behavior of the people in that environment, they will look out of place; thereby diminishing their level of covertness.

Say, for example, an operative wants to use a park bench at a block's distance from the target as a vantage point. What the operative would need to do is discover what type of people usually spend time on that bench, what these people look like, and how these people behave. The operative can then adjust their appearance and behavior in order to blend into this environment. But to do this, the operative will need to find a suitable location from which to collect information on the vantage point—in other words, a vantage point on the vantage point.

This second vantage point will ideally be a location from which the operative cannot even see the target because that would, in turn, mean that the target cannot see the operative either.

After spending some time observing the vantage point bench, if it turns out that it's usually occupied by homeless people, then the operative should adopt the cover of a homeless person—dressing and behaving in tune with the homeless people who usually occupy that bench. If the bench is usually occupied by business people, then the operative should adopt that type of cover, and so on. The idea is for the operative to act and appear in a way that would seem completely normal to others.

I often find myself in front of surprised security and law enforcement professionals (seasoned veterans in many cases) when I explain that they can no longer solely depend on the old-fashioned idea of detecting suspicious individuals who look out of place. The first thing a skilled surveillance operative will do is blend into their environment—that's what I was trained to do, and there's no reason to assume that others won't do the same.

As mentioned before, it's important to note that hostile surveillance isn't conducted for the fun of it. Instead, it serves as an important information collection tool for the type of hostile planning that leads to an attack. With this in mind, let's briefly cover the hostile planning process and give some much needed context to the subject of hostile surveillance.

THE HOSTILE PLANNING PROCESS

One way to very briefly sum up the hostile planning process is to cover the four progressive phases that lead up to an attack:

1. Initial collection of information. The main objective of this phase is to collect basic information on a number of potential targets in order to select the best one for an attack.

2. Analysis, planning, and training. This phase begins by collecting more detailed information on the selected target, locating its softest vulnerability, and putting together an action plan to exploit it. After the plan has been formulated, the next step is to make sure that the attack can be carried out according to this plan, which includes training, rehearsal, and advanced surveillance.

3. Execution. This phase covers the attack itself but also includes the last-minute surveillance that always precedes it.

4. Escape and exploitation. This phase comes after execution and is essentially the realization of the attack goals.

These simple and logical phases form the basic process that's used by almost every hostile entity—from shoplifters to bank robbers to terrorists. In fact, anyone who's spent time in the military might also recognize these phases since they're used in military operations as well.

Individuals and groups (regardless of their agendas) tend to follow the same patterns when faced with a challenge. This is precisely why understanding this process is so important. Only after we have abolished the mysteries behind hostile planning and hostile surveillance will we be able to effectively eliminate most of the guesswork from detection and prevention efforts.

With that in mind, let's take a look at some of the detection and prevention efforts we can employ against hostile surveillance.

STRATEGIES AGAINST HOSTILE SURVEILLANCE

San Francisco, 2011. A small conference room at the global headquarters of a Silicon Valley corporation.

The new global security director had invited me over to discuss the protective strategies he had in mind for the future. Our conversation centered around the subject of how best to secure the company's global headquarters in San Francisco. As in most cases, the building had a pretty conventional guard force; one that the new security director saw as inadequate.

"I want to upgrade the whole program," the director said. "Campus security is pretty much where it's going to be. I don't think I can expect much more from them [the conventional security guards], but I'm concerned about hostile surveillance with all the new threats we've been getting since our IPO. I want you guys to give me counter surveillance coverage."

The leap that many people try to make from conventional campus security to counter surveillance operations is actually a pretty common one. Needless to say—or not so needless to say, in many cases—it doesn't quite work that way, and it often falls to me to explain things and to recommend a good course of action.

Surveillance is a wide, deep, and varied field, which in turn means that the strategies we can employ against it are equally complex and varied. A good way to make sense of things is to divide the strategies into four general categories: attack deterrence, surveillance deterrence, surveillance detection, and counter surveillance.

Attack Deterrence

Attack deterrence is a preventive security measure that is most often carried out by a security guard force. The general idea is to paint an unwelcoming picture for hostile surveillance to see. As the hostile entity covertly collects information, security officers try to make it clear that the target in question is not an easy or desirable one, making it more probable that the hostile entity will either abandon its plan or take it elsewhere.

This simple yet effective strategy doesn't require any specialized training in surveillance detection. Instead, it can just as easily be achieved through strong visible security presence; breaking of routines (whenever possible); creating physical barriers; implementing access control procedures; and generally maintaining a high level of awareness, vigilance, and professionalism.

In some cases, concealing the access control process (the security function that controls who may enter) can also help harden the target. The idea is that hiding this process will make it harder for hostile surveillance to collect information on it—thereby making it harder to formulate a plan to get around security.

Another effective if somewhat less conventional strategy that can help deter hostile planners is to engage in activities that are difficult for the hostile surveillance entity to understand. For example, randomly photographing certain areas and people around the target or sporadically writing down license plate numbers of random vehicles in the area can help throw hostile operatives off their game. While this may seem confusing at first, the random nature of these actions is precisely the point. When observing these types of activities, hostile surveillance operatives are not likely to assume that they are performed for no good reason, which might compel them to try to understand these actions better. The simple act of trying to understand such random activities will, at the very least, lengthen the process of surveillance for them—causing the hostile entity to assume more risk. This shifting of the cost/risk benefit ratio should further increase the probability that the hostile entity will either abandon its plan or take it to a different target that can be more easily understood.

The inability of security personnel to identify hostile surveillance does not mean that the target is left completely vulnerable. And many people who accuse security forces of partaking in "security theater" miss this point. While this strategy might not guarantee safety (nothing actually can), it makes it much more likely that the hostile entity will simply select a less challenging target as it follows its hostile planning process.

Surveillance Deterrence

Surveillance deterrence takes the concept of attack deterrence and adds another layer to it—one that provides the appearance of an active attempt to expose surveillance. This doesn't actually mean that all security personnel must be trained in surveillance detection; it's enough that it *appears* that way in order to make it much harder or less desirable for a hostile surveillance operative to conduct surveillance on the target.

Surveillance deterrence can be achieved through a number of actions that will be viewed unfavorably by hostile surveillance operatives. Perhaps the most basic of these is an active projection of visual control over the area around the target, along with an attempt to detect and acknowledge any person spending time in the area, or even just passing through it (regardless of whether or not they seem suspicious).

It's important that a particularly large amount of attention be paid to the vantage points around the target. These vantage points can be located, assessed, and plotted out by a surveillance detection professional performing a service called *surveillance mapping*.

After surveillance mapping is complete, conventional security officers—not even necessarily well-trained ones, as is often the case—can be instructed to pay close attention to these locations. Their instructions should include random visits to these vantage points, performed as often as possible, along with casual acknowledgements and even polite verbal engagement with people who occupy them (regardless of whether or not they appear suspicious).

Keep in mind that a well-trained surveillance operative would probably assume a vantage point only after having established a solid cover and cover story, making it unlikely that they will be exposed by a conventional security officer. Nevertheless, when even a skilled surveillance operative is observed, acknowledged, and verbally engaged, it raises the probability that the hostile entity will either abandon its plan or take it to a different location where it will not be detected, much less acknowledged and engaged.

Surveillance Detection

Surveillance detection (SD) is the attempt to covertly determine if hostile surveillance is being conducted, and if so, to collect general information on the hostile surveillance entity (time, location, appearance, actions, and correlation to the target).

SD operations must be conducted in a covert manner—every bit as covert as hostile surveillance, if not more—because the person who is being detected might also be trained in covert methodology. For this reason, no connection between the SD operator and the target, or the target's security force, should be apparent.

In order to detect the subtle indicators of hostile surveillance, SD operators must first be well-versed in surveillance operations themselves. Generally speaking, these indicators consist of various types of subtle correlations to the target, and possibly some subtle mistakes that might only be apparent to an SD operator who knows what to look for (something we will discuss more deeply in Chapter 6). It's very possible that the detection of these subtle indicators will take quite a bit of time and require a number of fully dedicated SD operators, which is one of the reasons why SD operations are so costly and relatively rare. However, in recent years, as more public and private organizations have begun to understand the value of SD, it has become much more common than it used to be.

Counter Surveillance

Counter surveillance (CS) is a follow-up measure that is taken only after hostile surveillance has been detected. CS basically turns the tables by conducting surveillance on the surveillance. It must therefore be conducted in at least as covert a manner as SD, if not more so, since CS will probably need to observe, and possibly follow, hostile surveillance for even longer periods of time.

Counter surveillance is even riskier and more costly than SD, and will usually be conducted in order to discover who the hostile surveillance entity works for and to collect evidence for an arrest, litigation, and so on.

Now that we've covered the basics of hostile surveillance and provided some context for the measures we can employ against it, let's move on to explore the topic of mobile surveillance.

CHAPTER 5

MOBILE SURVEILLANCE

September, 2012.
A café in Palo Alto,
California.

Two men were sitting at a table and talking. One of the men was a former sales executive who had very recently been let go by a global IT corporation. The other man was the CEO and founder of the company. Unbeknown to both men, two covert operators were also in the café—one sitting at a table a few feet behind the CEO and another at a table behind the former executive.

The former executive was known to be belligerent at times, which was part of the reason he got himself fired. But he also had a professional relationship of some years with the CEO, which is why the CEO agreed to meet with him at a café just outside the corporate headquarters. The company's human resources director, who was informed of the upcoming meeting, was much less comfortable with it, which was the reason he contracted us to covertly protect the CEO.

The operator behind the CEO was me. I had covertly followed him there from the moment he left the corporate headquarters. The second operator had taken position in the café earlier on and was seated at a table with his laptop behind the former executive. (The backpack he brought the laptop in also contained emergency medical response equipment.) The meeting, which lasted around thirty minutes, had a few stressful moments, but it eventually ended without incident. As the two men parted ways, I stayed back to keep an eye on the former executive while the second operator covertly followed the CEO back to the corporate headquarters.

The reason we switched roles was to prevent too much direct correlation between ourselves and the two executives. The CEO arrived safely at the headquarters, and the second operator took a covert position outside the main entrance. I kept my eye on the former executive, who left the café and walked down a nearby alleyway which put him about half a block away from the main entrance to the corporate headquarters. He then decided to stick around at the end of the alley, nervously smoking two cigarettes while fiddling with his cellphone. It wasn't looking particularly good, and from my position at the other end of the alley, I communicated this to the second operator who was still covering the corporate headquarters.

After a tense fifteen minutes of this, the former exec exited the alley and started walking away from the headquarters. Although this was what we hoped he would do, we knew of past cases where disgruntled individuals only leave the scene in order to get a weapon from their vehicle, so I decided to covertly follow the former exec in order to find out if he was leaving the area for good.

Mobile surveillance on a potential hostile individual is different from the type of closer, protective surveillance we conducted on the CEO, and the distances I had to maintain from the former exec were much greater. I eventually ended my surveillance when he reached a train station a good two miles away from the headquarters.

It was quite a stroll...

UNDERSTANDING MOBILE SURVEILLANCE

Since the abovementioned operation included a good amount of mobile surveillance, let's go over some basics.

The general idea behind surveilling a mobile target is to see where the target goes and what they do. When this work is conducted by a single surveillance operative, it usually means that the surveillant wants to be somewhere *behind* the target. This gives the surveillant two advantages: 1) being able to see where the target is going, and 2) being out of the target's field of vision.

Taking it one level higher, the surveillant will also want to hide the fact that they are surveilling the target from anyone else in the area. This means that it's not enough to simply stay out of the target's field of vision as you duck behind garbage cans or quickly scurry between bus stops, trees, and dark corners. If your actions seem strange or suspicious to anyone around you, then you probably shouldn't do them.

One good way to covertly follow a target is to do so from the other side of the street where, in addition to being behind the target, you're also at a lateral angle to it. This not only raises your covertness level, but it also improves your ability to see where the target is going.

Many people might not realize this, but there are disadvantages to doing mobile surveillance directly behind a target. Walking directly behind someone makes it easier for the people around you (and for the target themself, if they turn around) to notice what you're doing. Secondly, if the target quickly turns a corner or walks into a store, they can suddenly disappear from your field of vision.

If, however, surveillance is conducted from the opposite side of the street, you not only maintain a higher level of covertness, but you also have a much wider angle and better field of vision on the target's side of the street. At the same time, the drawback of being on the other side of the street is that the added distance, traffic, and time that separates you from your target can be disadvantageous in very busy areas.

As always, the environment will end up determining the best way to approach the operation and what the best surveillance positions might be. So let's go ahead and delve into things a bit more deeply.

Distance and Speed

Surveillance is a tug-of-war game: pulling on one side is the need to observe the target as closely as possible and pulling on the other side is the need to keep cover and distance in order to maintain covertness. Balancing the tension between these opposing factors is hard enough in static situations, but when things go mobile, a new, challenging, and constantly shifting dimension gets injected into the mix.

One convenient thing about the environment-to-distance ratio is that environments where the target needs to be followed more closely (busy areas, for example) also tend to provide more cover, so the surveillant can stay closer. Conversely, quiet areas, which force the surveillant to keep their distance from the target, also provide an easier environment to keep track of the target from a longer distance.

Another aspect of the environment to take into account is that if the target has just started walking down a city block (or any other straightforward path), you can afford to be farther away from them since you can anticipate that they won't likely make any unexpected turns. But as the target nears the next intersection, you will want to get a bit closer to them so that you don't miss a turn if one is taken. Once you've reached the turn, you can slow down again—giving the target more distance—until they near the next intersection where you'll want to get closer again.

In addition to the environment, your distance from the target will also depend on the purpose of your mission. For example, if your surveillance has a protective function (like we maintained on the CEO in the opening story), the question becomes, "How close can I be to the protectee while still maintaining my cover?" Conversely, if your surveillance doesn't have a protective function (as was the case with the former exec), the question becomes, "How far can I afford to be from the target while making sure not to lose them?"

An important reason for maintaining the longest distance you can afford is that it can help you when the target makes short stops (for example, standing at a red light or stopping to check their phone). This distance buys the surveillant more time—time during which you can remain mobile after your target has transitioned to static mode.

If the distance and speed you're keeping allows it, you can often remain mobile for the duration of the target's short stop. The point is to avoid a situation where you're directly correlating to the target by stopping and going when the target stops and goes. A useful analogy is the distance you can keep from the vehicle in front of you while driving. If the distance is large enough, you can maintain a constant speed despite the fact that the car in front of you might keep stopping and going unexpectedly. The discrepancy between the consistent movement of the surveillant and the erratic stop-and-go movement of the target can help mask the surveillant's correlation to the target.

Longer Stops

When your target makes a longer stop, this can be a tricky situation because you don't usually know it's coming. In fact, if you knew about the stop ahead of time, you wouldn't have to conduct mobile surveillance in the first place—you would just wait for your target at their future stop location. The difficulty comes from the fact that you have to unexpectedly transition from mobile to static surveillance for an unknown length of time before possibly having to transition back to mobile when your target gets moving again.

Because the timing, location, and duration of these stops are unknown to you, acting naturally, maintaining cover, and not directly correlating to your target becomes very difficult. Remember, preserving your cover usually means that you must visually justify your presence by doing something that fits the environment and that is seemingly unrelated to the target. Sometimes this is simple (if, for example, there's a conveniently located coffee shop you can naturally walk into and use as a vantage point). At other times, however, it can prove very difficult (like when your target walks into a store that's surrounded by private residences). But either way, you'll have to literally think on your feet, do it quickly, and not draw attention to yourself as you do it.

There's no formula for where you should stop after the target has stopped, but you can make better decisions if you know the area in advance. It's also a good practice to constantly look ahead while moving, keeping an eye out for potential stop justifications. If you can look a block ahead of where you are at any given time, you can more naturally flow into a store or café that you spotted there if the need suddenly arises.

Ultimately, what you want to avoid are the unexpected "Oh shit" moments of shuffling double-takes or nervous stop-and-go movements that could correlate with your target when they make an unexpected stop. The correct way to handle such situations is to act like nothing happened (thereby blurring your correlation to the target). Keep on walking, find a store or café to stop in, invent a reason to check your phone, or come up with any other justification to stop that's seemingly unrelated to the target's stop. Keep in mind that this justification should ideally match the length of time you predict the target will remain static. If the target walks into a convenience store, you probably don't have to be static for all that long. But if the target walks into a nice restaurant, your stop justification might have to be longer.

Just like with short stops, here too, maintaining a longer distance from your target can help blur your correlation by stretching more time between your target's transition from mobile to static and your own. But don't overstretch things by walking back and forth in the area before finally transitioning to static position since this might call more attention to you rather than less. You want to stretch the time between the target's transition and yours, but don't *overstretch* it.

This works the same way when the transition is from static to mobile. If, for example, your target exits a building and starts walking down the street, you would be wise to let the target get a good half a block away before you also make the same inevitable transition from static to mobile. But here, too, don't overstretch it or you might end up losing your target.

Observing the Target's Body Language

Much of the difficulty in surveillance comes from the fact that you don't know what the target's next move will be. A useful way to mitigate some of this difficulty is to notice your target's body language. People will often project their intentions before they're about to do something, and if you're observant enough to pick up on these projections, you can anticipate their actions *before* they happen.

For example, people usually look and move towards the direction they intend to go. So if, for example, your target looks and moves a bit to the left as they near an intersection, they'll probably end up turning left. Likewise, if your target is sitting at a coffee shop and starts collecting their things, putting their cell phone in their pocket, etc. they're probably getting ready to leave—thereby transitioning to mobile.

Any advanced knowledge you can attain about your target's movements is extremely useful (even if it's just a few seconds in advance). Ultimately, this foreshadowing can help avoid surprises and better prepare you for inevitable transitions.

TEAMWORK

Up to this point, I've mostly focused on how to single-handedly conduct mobile surveillance. However, working in a team is far more effective and is actually the ideal way to conduct mobile surveillance. Not only does teamwork make it easier to keep track of a target, but it also minimizes the risks of being detected.

One useful technique that a team can employ is leapfrogging their surveillance behind or around a target. This is achieved when the surveillant who's following a target is replaced by a new surveillant who comes in from behind or who is waiting somewhere up ahead. When executed correctly, the first surveillant peels off the pursuit as the new one takes their place. This leapfrog move can be repeated and will effectively blur the correlations between any single individual and the target.

At the same time, leapfrogging can also make transitions from mobile to static (or vice versa) less noticeable. For example, if the target transitions from mobile to static, the mobile surveillant who followed the target to that point can report where the target has stopped and keep going. A fresh team member (one who didn't just follow the target) can then glide into the scene and conduct static surveillance. As the target transitions back to mobile again, the static surveillant reports this, and another team member (one who wasn't static in the immediate area) can go mobile after the target.

A more complex way for a team to conduct mobile surveillance is by maintaining a "floating box" around the target. This virtual box is achieved by having team members surround the target on all sides. Team members can, for example, be behind the target and in front of them (on both sides of the street), and possibly on parallel streets to the right and left of the target as well. Obviously, the members of this team must be in very good communication with each other (covertly, of course) as this "box" continuously moves with the target. If the target makes a turn off the street they were on, the roles of the team members in the box can shift around in order to avoid the appearance of the target being followed by any single individual.

A FEW EXTRA TAKEAWAYS FROM THE OPERATION

Now that we've covered the basics of mobile surveillance, I'd like to turn our attention back to the opening story about the CEO and former executive. Although a café meeting between two people might seem simple, planning a covert protective detail is more complex than most people think.

For starters, the café meeting was between two individuals who were coming from two different directions, and who were to be kept in the dark about our presence. We obviously couldn't coordinate anything with them and the only known factors we had to go on were the start time and location for the meeting.

Once the meeting was over, we made an educated guess that the CEO would go back to the headquarters the same way he came to the café (because that's what people usually do), but we had no real idea where the former exec would go. This meant our plan had to be as detailed as possible, but it also had to be simple and flexible enough to roll with the punches.

We approached the operation by conducting advanced walk-throughs to cover both relevant locations (the corporate headquarters and the café), all access points, possible routes, side streets, and vantage points. We also met with the corporate headquarters' security manager in order to coordinate, establish lines of operational communications and to get photos of the CEO and the former executive so we could recognize them.

As it turned out, the first curveball came right at the beginning of the operation. During the planning stage, the headquarters' security manager had insisted that the operation begin with the second operator (the one inside the café) covertly communicating to him when the former exec showed up. The security manager would then let the CEO know that he was good to go for his meeting, and he would then notify us when the CEO was about to exit the building.

I already had my doubts about this plan, which seemed overly

Surveillance Zone

complex and depended not only on factors outside of our control, but also on a security manager who was not trained and experienced in these types of operations. For this reason, the second operator and I had prepared for the possibility that things would not actually get started that way—which is precisely what happened.

Instead of walking into the café, the former exec decided to wait for the CEO outside the café, which meant that the second operator sitting inside couldn't see him and report to the security manager when he arrived. Additionally, the security manager, who did not position himself very well, failed to notice when the CEO was about to exit the headquarters. And when the CEO did eventually leave, nothing was conveyed to us.

Training and experience had taught me that the initial transition from static surveillance to mobile is always a crucial one, and I had taken a good vantage point outside the headquarters for this reason. My first realization that the operation had begun was when I caught a glimpse of the CEO as he exited the headquarters and started walking towards the café.

It's often said that luck favors the well prepared, which is another way of saying that you make your own luck. I had studied the CEO's photo so well that I immediately recognized him, even though I had never met the man before and I could only see the back of his head as he exited the building.

I followed him relatively closely, and when the CEO got to the café, the second operator, who was already inside the café, communicated to me that the two men had just walked in and were getting coffee without incident. I held back about fifty feet outside the café and entered a few minutes later to avoid directly correlating to the CEO's movements. I ordered a cup of coffee and sat down at the table behind the CEO. My teammate had been closely watching the two the whole time they were in the café.

When the meeting was over, the CEO went back to the headquarters (with the second operator following closely after him). That went pretty much as expected. What we had not expected was that the sales exec would go into the alleyway next to the café and hang out there.

Nevertheless, because we had conducted a thorough advance of the whole area, we knew the alley well and knew exactly where it led. The holding pattern we had to maintain—with me covering the former exec in the alley and the second operator covering the entrance to the headquarters—was not the scenario we were hoping for, but it was certainly a possibility we were prepared for.

Fortunately, our operation ended successfully with all mission parameters being achieved—everyone went home safely and security was maintained throughout the operation. Ultimately, because proper covert field craft was applied, reputations were maintained and potential public relations problems were averted. This example clearly shows how solid preparation, good communication, a simple plan, and a flexible disposition can result in an effective mobile surveillance operation and a positive result for everyone involved.

Now that we've covered the various types of static and mobile surveillance, in the next chapters, we're going to switch gears and delve into surveillance detection.

CHAPTER 6

HOSTILE SURVEILLANCE DETECTION

San Francisco, 2013. An important shareholders meeting. Annual shareholders meetings usually get a fair amount of security, including even metal detector screening, but this was no typical meeting.

The corporation in question had gotten itself into a bit of legal and public relations trouble, and this being San Francisco, things were getting "interesting." The shareholders who arrived at the meeting had to pass through a circus of protesters, reporters, and people both protesting *and* reporting who like to call themselves "freelance reporters" (better known as bloggers).

Unbeknownst to all was the fact that security on the venue had started days earlier. The main concern wasn't about the normal protesters and reporters who were kind enough to make their presence known. No, the concern was about those who might secretly *surveil* the venue, possibly even using the protest as a distraction, in order to figure out a way to circumvent security and penetrate the event. For this reason, all the locations that could be used as vantage points on the venue were being covertly monitored by up to three operators at a time.

We were essentially looking for people who were engaged in hostile surveillance—similar to the activities I myself conducted during the Red-Team exercise in Chapter 4. As I explained earlier, the idea behind role-playing a hostile surveillant is to discover security vulnerabilities. I had done this days earlier for this event, and my next step was to figure out where the potential hostile surveillance vantage points might be. In other words, where would I position myself if I were a hostile surveillant? My final step before the operation was to plan out where our surveillance detection team members should position themselves in order to detect potential hostile surveillants.

UNDERSTANDING SURVEILLANCE DETECTION

Surveillance detection (SD) is *the attempt to covertly determine whether surveillance is being conducted, and if so, to collect general information on the surveillance entity.*

Before I introduce the fundamentals of surveillance detection, I would first like to make some general clarifications about the subject:

- **The field of surveillance detection is both wide and deep.** Many of its fundamental principles admit of some exceptions to the rules, and even of exceptions to the exceptions. As such, the purpose of this chapter is to provide a very general introduction, not a detailed rundown of the countless details and case-by-case contingencies that exist.

- **You can't learn how to perform surveillance detection from a book.** These are skills that can only be acquired through field training and operational experience. And while some of the wording here might seem instructional, please keep in mind that this is primarily for the sake of illustrating the concepts, not teaching how to employ them.

Over the years, I've found that a good way to explain surveillance detection is by breaking it down into its two basic components:

1. Understanding what to look for—What is it about other people that needs to be detected?

2. Understanding how to look and from where—What is it about the SD operator that enables them to detect surveillance, and where should they position themselves to do so?

With these concepts in mind, let's take a closer look at what it takes to effectively detect hostile surveillance.

WHAT TO LOOK FOR

Many people tend to think that to detect hostile surveillance you should spot anyone who seems suspicious, out of place, or nervous and that you should look for people taking a special interest in the protected target (for example, intently observing, taking notes, photographing, videotaping, and so on). While these factors might very well exist, it's also important to note that obvious indicators like these will only be detected if low-level surveillance is being carried out. In other words, the very first thing that a skilled surveillance operative learns is how *not* to display any of the above indicators.

When it comes to detecting surveillance (on any level), the single most important indicator to look for is *correlation to the target*. If the term *correlation* seems a bit vague, that's because it is. In fact, this ambiguity is one of the reasons why surveillance can be quite difficult to detect—especially at the higher levels where correlations are extremely subtle.

In general, a correlation can be any act of observing, moving, signaling, or communicating—or even just presence over time and distance—which is done in conjunction with the target. And though there are ways to blur and camouflage these types of correlations, with the exception of a few rare cases, there is no real way to completely eliminate them while still conducting effective physical surveillance.

The best way to understand what correlations to a target might look like, and why they almost always exist when surveillance is carried out, is to experience how it actually *feels* to conduct surveillance yourself (something we discussed in Chapter 4). After you've experienced how surveillance feels in the flesh, you will be much better positioned to spot people who are going through the same experience.

In much the same way, many casinos and fraud detection units have been known to hire ex-cheats, frauds, and con artists *precisely because* they're extremely adept at detecting the very same tricks they themselves used to employ. In order to catch or detect a criminal, you have to think like one.

As you'll recall from Chapter 4, I explained that the hostile surveillance process begins by understanding the area around a target and locating potential vantage points. To summarize, a *vantage point* is any location from which the operative can conduct surveillance on a target, and a good surveillance vantage point is one that gives the operative access to important visual information while allowing them to appear as though they're a natural part of the environment.

What makes surveillance so difficult, however, is that as seemingly normal as an operative might strive to appear, the fact will always remain that there's a constant tension—a conflict—between their *appearance* and *what they're actually doing*. And it is within the scope of what the operative is *actually doing*—visually collecting information on the target—that most surveillance correlations can be found.

If a surveillance operative is trying to visually collect information on a target, then as natural as their actions may seem, correlations to the target are almost inevitable: The simple act of looking at a target is a correlation. Moving in conjunction with the target, in order to not lose track of it, is another type of correlation. Paying close attention to the target at key moments can also be a type of correlation. Signaling, gesturing, telephoning, texting, or even just checking the time in conjunction with a target's movements or activities can also be a correlation.

Another type of correlation to the target, a particularly difficult one to detect, is what's called *correlation over time and distance*. For example, if the target is a CEO who is staying at a hotel for a week, this correlation can be something as subtle as an individual spending every morning in that hotel lobby for the duration of that week. Even if the individual doesn't directly correlate to the target in any of the abovementioned ways, the simple presence of the individual over that specific time period is called a *correlation over time*.

If the CEO happens to be on a multi-city business trip, and the same individual in question is seen spending time in the lobby of each hotel the CEO is staying at (say, in New York, London, and Tokyo), their mere presence in each of these hotels, at the same time the CEO happens to be there, can be a *correlation over time and distance*.

A useful analogy for correlation over time and distance is the *Where's Waldo* game (or *Where's Wally* if you're more familiar with the original UK version). Trying to find the title character inside an elaborate picture puzzle pretty much encapsulates the idea of detecting correlations over time and distance. The difficulty when it comes to SD, however, is that you don't know *who* Waldo is or what he looks like.

Surveillance Zone

WHERE TO LOOK FROM

Now that we generally understand what to look for, the question becomes where should we look from? The way to answer this question is to realize that a correlation, not unlike an equation, has two sides to it: the target and the surveillance operative. An ideal way to establish whether a correlation exists is to see *both* sides of the correlation—*simultaneously*, if possible. In order to do this, and to remain hidden from the surveillance operative, the ideal SD vantage point will be somewhere *behind* the surveillance vantage point.

For example, if a bench at the edge of a park is recognized as a good surveillance vantage point on an important building nearby, a potential SD vantage point might be a bench further back in the park overlooking both the first bench and the building. Another example of a surveillance vantage point might be a window seat inside a coffee shop (where a surveillant can look out the window at their target). In that case, a potential SD vantage point can be a seat in the back of that coffee shop where an SD operator can see the individuals looking out the coffee shop window.

It's important to remember that convenient notions of ideal SD situations (like the ones I just mentioned) aren't always available, and one of the most important purposes of field training is to learn how to deal with less than optimal conditions while still getting the job done.

SURVEILLANCE INDICATORS

Downtown Oakland, California. 2010.

The CEO's meeting with his friend and prospective client was scheduled to take place at a well-known café. Unfortunately, the CEO's friend, who had a large social media following, tweeted about their upcoming meeting. In response, the CEO's protective intelligence analyst who picked up on this tweet, advised the CEO to cancel his now-publicized meeting.

However, the CEO not only insisted on still meeting his friend but also on doing so without a protective detail. The company's head of executive protection, who was not thrilled about this idea, decided to secretly deploy a surveillance detection team in and around the café, which would covertly look for any signs of hostile surveillance on the CEO.

When the CEO walked into the café, his friend was already waiting for him at a table next to the window. Sitting in the back of the café was a member of the surveillance detection team. As the CEO walked in, the SD operator noticed that a middle-aged man who was looking at the CEO proceeded to pull out his phone and type something into it.

After sitting and talking for twenty minutes, the CEO and his friend decided to exit the café and take a short walk. The SD operator in the back of the café once again noticed that the middle-aged man typed something into his phone before exiting the café about thirty seconds behind the CEO and his friend. This information was immediately communicated to the other members of the surveillance detection team who were in position outside. The other team members were then able to observe both the CEO and the middle-aged man who was now following him on the street.

This is one of many scenarios I have my trainees practice in our surveillance detection courses. It's often the instructors who role-play the CEO and his friend and an experienced contractor who role-plays the hostile surveillance operative. It's the job of the trainees to plan and execute the operation, which they are then evaluated on.

To get an idea of just how subtle surveillance indicators (or correlations) can be, try to imagine our last scenario—the café meeting between the CEO and his friend—*without* it focusing on a specific middle-aged man. If you consider the fact that most of us have phones in our hands much of the time, one out of any number of individuals holding their phones in a busy café should not seem the least bit suspicious. And yet, grabbing a cellphone could be all it takes to communicate, take note, or even photograph a target. What an SD operator needs to do is notice the timing of such subtle actions (at the arrival and departure of the target), and the location from which they're done (a table that provides a logical surveillance vantage point). Surveillance indicators can be very subtle, and this means that SD requires a very subtle eye.

As discussed earlier, a correlation over time and/or distance is the mere *presence* of the same individual (or possibly a number of individuals) in the vicinity of the target. No direct observation, communication, photography, movement, or even subtle correlative gestures are detected, and yet there the person is—over and over again—in different times and places where the target just happens to be.

This can be very difficult to detect because it's not so much a matter of visual observation as it is the ability to *notice* and *keep track of* people. If, for example, you're conducting SD on an important CEO, you'll need to notice that one individual, out of a roomful of people around the CEO, is the same individual who also happened to be in a roomful of people around the CEO a few hours ago—and who might have also been on the street outside the CEO's residence yesterday.

In order to detect these types of correlation, you'll need to memorize or list all the individuals who have occupied potential vantage points around the target during the day—regardless of whether or not they correlated in action—and later on compare those individuals to future individuals in different times and locations around the target. If any of these people come up as common denominators more than once or twice, this might indicate that a correlation is happening.

When you start to pay such close attention to people, I can assure you that there will be an abundance of false-positive detections. Keep in mind that people—all people—tend to be creatures of habit. The same individual looking out of a coffee shop window every morning is worth noting to be sure, but this has to be balanced out with the fact that every coffee shop has its regulars, who often like to sit at the same tables. And while experience might help clear out some of the white noise, there is no magic formula that can guarantee you won't get false positives.

One useful tip, at least when it comes to correlations over time and distance, is that it takes a minimum of three instances to establish a pattern. So if you see the same person once again, it's a coincidence. If you see them twice, that elevates it to suspicious. And three times can elevate it to a correlation. This is imperfect to be sure, but it gives you something to start with.

Hostile surveillance detection is an endless cat-and-mouse game, with the added difficulty of not knowing who the cats and mice are—or if they're even present. It's a game with very loose rules, if any, but it does have some general principles that can help you understand how it's played.

In the next chapter, we're going to really get things moving and hop aboard the roller coaster that is *mobile* surveillance detection.

CHAPTER 7
MOBILE SURVEILLANCE DETECTION

Downtown San Jose, California. 2011.

After sitting comfortably for a while in the beautiful lobby of the Fairmont hotel, I decided to take a little stroll around downtown and get a cappuccino at a nice café.

As I got up from my comfortable seat, a man who was sitting on the far side of the lobby raised his head and watched me walk towards the exit. The man then followed me out of the hotel and stayed behind me (at a safe distance) during my entire stroll and cappuccino break.

If you've read this far into the book, you're probably guessing (correctly) that someone was also there to detect my surveillant. I was actually taking part in a surveillance detection (SD) field exercise. My job was to role-play an executive visiting Silicon Valley who was suspected of being under surveillance. A team of SD trainees were spread out at key locations (or SD vantage points) in and around the

Fairmont hotel, trying to detect if anyone was following me. The man who *was* following me, and who the SD trainees were trying to detect, was a hostile surveillance role-player.

UNDERSTANDING MOBILE SURVEILLANCE DETECTION

When you first read a story like this and try to imagine how you would detect a hostile surveillance operative, it sounds pretty straightforward—maybe even easy. After all, the hostile surveillant is following your protected client (also known as *principal*) all around the downtown area, so why would it be difficult to detect such a thing?

But the truth is mobile surveillance detection is much trickier than most people imagine, and unless the hostile surveillant is right on top of their target, even a controlled exercise like the one above can be quite a challenge. This is even true for trainees with years of experience in Special Forces, law enforcement, and security (as was the case above). These exercises usually need to be repeated over and over again until the SD trainees develop the type of sensitivity that's necessary for detecting mobile surveillance. In the San Jose exercise, it took four consecutive strolls (with four cappuccinos in my stomach) before the trainees finally detected that I had been followed the entire time.

Similar to previous chapters, I'm discussing mobile surveillance and surveillance detection as they're conducted on foot—rather than in vehicles. There are a couple of reasons for this. First, the general principles are pretty similar, and the concepts of mobile surveillance and SD are much easier to illustrate using non-vehicular examples. And second, I'm much more experienced in surveillance and SD on foot and therefore feel more qualified to talk about this arena.

When it comes to mobile surveillance, there are two general categories to consider:

1. **Mobile surveillance on a static target.** This is our attempt to detect a hostile surveillant that's moving in the vicinity of a static target, usually because there are no good static vantage points from which to conduct surveillance.

2. **Mobile surveillance on a moving target.** This is our attempt to detect a hostile surveillant that's moving in conjunction with a mobile target.

Because we've already discussed SD on static targets in the last chapter, let's move on to SD on mobile targets.

What to Look For

As we've seen in earlier chapters, detecting hostile surveillance is a matter of detecting *correlation to the target*—that is, spotting individuals who correlate to the target in movement, observation, action, or presence. In Chapter 5, I discussed various ways in which hostile surveillants can blur and mask these correlations, but these tactics will not eliminate them. And if you know where to look, what to look for, when to look for it, and where to look from, you stand a better chance of detecting these subtle or skillfully blurred correlations.

Where to Look

One of the main reasons we need to learn how to conduct surveillance before we delve into surveillance detection is so we can understand where to look for it. The simple answer here is that you should look for surveillance at the locations where you yourself would be if you were the one conducting surveillance. And when it comes to mobile surveillance, the surveillant will usually want to be somewhere *behind* the target, and possibly behind and to the side of the street.

So as the target moves forward on a typical city sidewalk, we can visualize surveillance "Red Zones" that follow them. These are areas where you can reasonably expect to find a mobile surveillant. Typically, this includes one zone behind the target (stretched out for about half a block or so) and another behind them but on the opposite side of the street. These Red Zones will essentially be "dragged" behind the target as it moves forward, which means we'd want to keep track of who's in these zones.

An important time to look for correlations to the target is when a *change of direction* is made. For example, if the target takes a right turn, notice who else takes that same right turn shortly after (within the timeframe you would expect someone in the Red Zone to reach the turn). The more turns or changes in direction the target makes, the more opportunities you'll have to spot someone who keeps correlating. This same idea also applies when the target stops moving, thereby transitioning from mobile to static.

Learning how to deal with stops is something we'll discuss in a moment, but first, let's take a look at distance and speed as they relate to conducting mobile SD.

Distance and Speed

As we discussed in Chapter 5, the distance and speed the surveillant would want to maintain in relation to the target will depend on several factors, including: the target's movements, the environment, the people in the area, and the surveillance goals. Knowing this, we can begin to make more educated guesses about the size, location, and proximity of the Red Zones—and about the people who are in them.

For example, if we notice that an individual who was walking half a block behind the target on a normal street shortens their distance to the target when the area becomes busier, this could indicate a correlation. Another example of a subtle correlation would be if the individual slows down and allows more distance between themselves and the target as they start walking down a city block, but then quickens their pace to get closer as the target nears the next intersection. The more times we see these back and forth changes in relative speed and distance, the better our chances of spotting a correlation to the target. This is essentially how we can begin to distinguish between coincidental correlations (which will always occur) and consistent trends that indicate an intentional correlation.

Short Stops

Any time the target makes a stop, we have an opportunity to spot a correlation because the hostile surveillant might also be forced to stop. Keep in mind that as soon as the target stops moving (thereby becoming a static target), the Red Zone—which was primarily dragged behind the target up to this point—can now spread itself into a radius that surrounds the target on all sides. This expands the options that a hostile surveillant has for justifying a stop or for buzzing around the area, which can make it harder to detect. But the more stops that are made, the easier it will become for a well-trained eye to spot that someone keeps correlating to the target. As subtle as these correlations may be, through repetition and careful observation, the patterns will start to emerge.

In Chapter 5, I discussed how inevitable "Oh shit" surveillance moments can be handled, both correctly and incorrectly, by a surveillant. Obviously, if the hostile surveillant mishandles a transition (which is not uncommon), correlations are easier to spot. For example, if the target makes an inevitable short stop (for something like a traffic light or to check their phone), a surveillant in the Red Zone might come to a nervously abrupt stop—thereby demonstrating not only a correlation of observation and movement, but even overt suspicious behavior.

However, if the hostile surveillant is a bit more skillful, they might be able to blur these correlations by pretending to stop and check their own phone, walking into a store for a few moments, passing the target and stopping up ahead, or moving around in the area until the target starts moving again.

Even so, the hostile surveillant's attempt to blur their correlations can never eliminate them completely, and a skilled SD operator who knows what to look for should still be able to identify these correlations by noticing that a specific individual intentionally keeps staying inside the surveillance Red Zone—over and over again.

Long Stops

I define long stops as locations that a mobile target reaches on purpose. These could include a scheduled meeting point, event venue, meal location, residence, workplace, school, or any other intentional destination. Because the target arrives at these locations on purpose, oftentimes for prescheduled reasons, the ideal situation is for the SD operators to be briefed on these scheduled stops in advance (thought it can still work without the briefing).

The reason prior knowledge is so helpful is because it can enable the SD operators to remain static in the area of the long stop, which will help them maintain a higher level of covertness while observing and noticing more themselves. This is the type of home-field advantage that SD operators might need if they are to uncover the actions of a skilled hostile surveillant.

As SD operators prepare (or advance) for a scheduled long stop, they should become well acquainted with the environment around the stop location, the type of traffic that flows in and out of the area, the type of people who spend time there, and most especially, the potential vantage points around the stop location. SD operators should be set up *before* the scheduled stop, and as the target arrives, every individual who arrives in the area within the next few minutes should be noted—suspicious or not.

Even if an individual is not seen looking at the target, their mere presence in relation to the target, over time and distance, can indicate a correlation. A single SD operator might not be able to connect all the dots (by noticing every single correlation), but with dedicated teamwork and careful attention to people, timing, and vantage points, subtle trends can emerge, indicating that there's a correlation.

Where to Look From

When it comes to choosing a location, surveillance detection is not all that different from surveillance. The actual locations chosen might be different, but the rules are essentially the same. Your location should enable you to:

1. Spot and observe a potential target.
2. Not be seen by the target, or identified as someone who is observing the target.

The primary difference between hostile surveillants and SD operators is *who* their target is. For the hostile surveillant, the protectee (often referred to as the *principal*) is the target. While for the SD operator, the hostile surveillant is the target.

For this reason, SD operators will want to position themselves where they can observe the surveillance Red Zone while remaining outside of it. Not only will this hide the SD operator from the hostile surveillant, but it will also help them detect correlations. This is because a correlation is easier to spot when you can see both sides of it, which means the SD operator would want to see both the protectee/principal *and* the hostile surveillant, simultaneously.

The ideal way to do this is by remaining static, which is why prior knowledge of the movements and destinations of the principal is so important. In this sense, the "mobile" part of mobile surveillance detection refers more to *what* you're trying to detect—the hostile surveillant—rather than to you, the SD operator who's doing the detecting.

In the last two chapters, I've essentially covered the mechanics of how surveillance detection works. What I want to do next is delve a bit deeper into the details and experiences of SD operations, share some insights based on my own experiences in the field, and give you a glimpse of how it actually feels to conduct surveillance detection.

CHAPTER 8

LESSONS FROM THE FIELD: SURVEILLANCE DETECTION

Santa Clara convention center, 2014. A large Silicon Valley conference was taking place, and I was the team leader for the surveillance detection contingency that was spread around the convention center. We had been hired to covertly detect and report anyone trying to surveil the event, and I was looking forward to working with a team I had personally trained and hand-picked for the operation.

On the face of it, leading a team of operators who you trained yourself is a great thing. There shouldn't be any surprises coming from them since everyone knows what to do and how to do it. But, as is often the case, good old reality has other plans in store for you, and before I knew it, in came a flood of false-positive reports and all manner of operational mistakes.

Yes, training was over, but on-the-job training was just beginning.

FIELD REALITY

I'll admit, it's a bit annoying to have to deal with issues you thought you'd trained your operators to avoid, but I keep reminding myself that training is *not* the same as real-life operations (something I too had to learn when I was first starting out).

As frustrating at this is, it is to be expected, and when you're out in the field, in real life, things are rarely ever simple and clean cut. This is why I've dedicated this chapter to some of the practical lessons I've learned over the years about the reality of SD operations.

BREAKING OLD HABITS

Old habits die hard. Many people (myself included) who go into surveillance detection have military, law enforcement, or security backgrounds, and it's hard to break the habits that had been so important to maintain up till that point. These old habits include: taking positions close enough to be in physical control of your client, projecting awareness and visual control, patrolling, and more.

One way to break out of these habits is to keep reminding ourselves that SD is not, strictly speaking, physical security. Instead, it falls into the realm of *protective intelligence*, and the distances, actions, and postures that need to be assumed should reflect that.

While it might feel odd at first to do things such as sit back and play with your phone (or at least pretend to) at some café a block away from your client, intelligence work has a different function from that of physical security. By showing such things as seriousness, awareness, and readiness to take action (which means falling back into old security habits) many operators ironically make themselves much *less* effective.

If the client wanted another strong and sharp protector, they would have hired one. SD operators are there to provide a function that security cannot—to be the eyes and ears that security cannot have and to detect and report what security cannot perceive.

CLOTHING

Most people who are told they're going to spend a considerable amount of time on a covert operation take this to mean they should "dress the part." I've seen trainees and operators go with jeans and dark hoodie combos, all black clothing, leather jackets, the "sunglasses with a baseball cap" classic, and all manner of tactical clothing and apparel. Unfortunately, these are not the best looks for the job.

Now would be the time to get any romantic notions of sharp-looking Hollywood secret agents out of your head. A private sector covert operator should look more like an administrative assistant on a lunch break than Jason Bourne on a mission.

I'm also not a fan of what's considered "covert-tactical" clothing and apparel, and I've seen plenty of operators try to pull that off too. For example, I often find myself telling operators not to use their favorite pair of tactical boots. (Yes, we can see what they are, and no, they don't just look like ordinary shoes—not even when they're half covered by your pant legs.) In fact, if the product has the word "Covert" anywhere in its title, it usually isn't. If it seems like a sharp piece of clothing or gear that you think will look good on you during a covert operation, you should probably leave it at home.

Okay, so that's some stuff you should avoid, but what do I suggest you actually wear?

For SD operations, I'm a big fan of the boring business-casual look (a business shirt tucked into slacks or khakis). One of the most useful aspects of this style is that it covers the widest range of environments and does so without looking suspicious or attention-grabbing. Business-casual easily blends into downtown/financial district environments, but it also works very well in residential areas—especially in quiet, high-end neighborhoods where people tend to be more suspicious of an unfamiliar person. The business-casual look works in most city parks, cafés, and restaurants (where most other appearances work as well), but it can also easily get you in and out of high-end hotels, stores, boutiques, galleries, and office or apartment building lobbies.

Of course, business-casual isn't a guaranteed pass into any location (nothing is), but on the whole it can give you the advantage of looking harmless and uninteresting to the widest range of people—from police officers on patrol to hotel lobby employees, shopkeepers, homeowners, and most people on the street. Last but not least, it will also make you less noticeable to hostile surveillants.

There's a bit of a range to what's considered business-casual, but what I mean by it is a buttoned-up business shirt tucked into slacks with dress shoes or possibly nice walking shoes. A full suit and tie will overshoot the mark and will make you more noticeable rather than less. You can scale down the look by replacing slacks with jeans, but make sure it's a nice pair. Don't wear sneakers or hiking shoes, and don't untuck that shirt. Those who know what to look for will immediately notice the combination of comfortable or sporty shoes with an untucked shirt (the kind that's good for concealing a weapon or radio).

So does this mean SD operators probably won't be able to conceal a weapon? Yes, it does, and I'm generally not a fan of carrying weapons when conducting SD. (Most clients actually insist on unarmed SD operators.) A weapon won't be necessary to protect anyone else since SD isn't physical security—it's field intelligence. And if an SD operator feels too uncomfortable going out on a covert operation unarmed, then I recommend they either work on improving that comfort level or reconsider whether private sector surveillance detection is the right fit for them.

Yes, it's true that lots of normal people out there walk around with jeans, hoodies, untucked shirts, baseball caps, sunglasses, and sporty or ruggedized footwear. But those people don't also have to worry about properly executing an SD operation, covertly occupying vantage points, spending hours on end in the same area and possibly having to wander in and out of stores, hotels, and office buildings.

Whenever there's a choice between appearing cool and operational or nerdy and boring, the latter should always win. The fact that this doesn't suit the taste of many people with law enforcement, military, or security backgrounds, and doesn't fit what most people imagine a covert operator should look like, is *exactly* the point. It's not about looking good—look good on your own time. During SD operations, you need to be bland and boring so no one notices or remembers you.

CORRELATION TO THE TARGET—YES OR NO?

We've discussed the idea of detecting correlations in previous chapters, and this fundamental rule of SD becomes very apparent when you're trying to determine the degree of suspicion you should attribute to an individual. There's a very natural tendency for people looking for hostile surveillance to start seeing lots of it. It's a classic form of confirmation bias—*"the tendency to search for, interpret, favor, and recall information in a way that confirms one's preexisting beliefs."*[1] When you start carrying a hammer, everything begins to look like a nail.

If you let your bias get the best of you, you're going to drown in a sea of false-positive detections—everyone around you will begin to look suspicious (especially in cities like San Francisco). This is when you need to remind yourself that the defining factor for surveillance detection is *correlation to the target*. No correlation to the target means no positive detection, and how strange someone's actions or appearance might seem to you won't change that.

SD is a pretty crazy business, and the hyperawareness that operators have to maintain can really play with your mind. I've seen operators get themselves worked up to the point of paranoia—reporting multiple positive detections of everything from hostile surveillance to

---

[1] Wikipedia contributors, "Confirmation bias," Wikipedia, The Free Encyclopedia, https://en.wikipedia.org/w/index.php?title=Confirmation_bias&oldid=733737210 (accessed August 14, 2016).

other mysterious SD units all around. I don't pretend to be completely immune to this. Practice and experience can certainly help sort things out, but the best way to calm the SD demons in your head and to stay on track with your mission is to simply ask, "Is there a correlation to the target, and if so, what is it?" If you can't answer this question or frame your suspicion in the context of correlating to the target, then you can't establish a positive detection. In such cases, you simply make a mental note of the person you're suspicious of and move on.

OVER-OBSERVING AND OVER-REPORTING

At the start of this chapter, I talked about leading a team of SD operators for a Silicon Valley conference. As it turns out, during the SD operation, my team did actually detect an individual correlating to the target. What we noticed was that this individual had been occupying two different vantage points for long periods of time—jumping back and forth between them in order to observe the main entrance of the convention center. The individual was initially detected and reported by me, and then later by two more team members. The problem was that these two team members then went on to continuously observe the suspect, follow him around, and send a flurry of minute-by-minute reports about every single movement (or non-movement) he was making. After a short while, I had to call them off and post them elsewhere.

It's not uncommon for SD operators to over observe and over-analyze activities like this. Once a person is found correlating to the target, it's very tempting for security-minded professionals (and I'm including myself here) to not let the suspect out of their sight and to keep collecting as many details about them as they can.

The problem with this is that the mission of an SD operator is to detect and report if hostile surveillance is being conducted—no more. This means that after a strong correlation is reported, it's not usually the job of the SD operator to sit on top of the suspect and keep collecting and reporting more and more details. That job might belong to counter surveillance or (more often than not) to conventional security or law enforcement who will engage the individual.

Unless the SD mission also includes a physical protection or counter surveillance component, your job is to report what you've detected, give a description of the individual and their correlations to the target, and then move on. It's not that you want to ignore them afterwards, on the contrary, you'll keep reporting if you see them correlating again in the future. But after the first time they've been detected and reported, there are sharply diminishing returns to hovering over them, and sharply increasing chances you'll get yourself detected as an SD operator if you do so.

Most clients are almost as worried about their SD operators getting exposed (and embarrassingly splattered all over social and conventional media) as they are about hostile surveillance itself. Report and move on!

FOLLOWING SUSPECTS

As the case above illustrates, I've found that SD operators (and, again, I'm not excluding myself from this) have a natural yet unfortunate inclination to follow suspects once they start moving away from a particular vantage point. In most cases, this is an unnecessary and risky move that should be avoided.

As you'll recall from Chapters 5 and 7, the only reason to perform mobile surveillance on a mobile individual is if we don't know where they're going. But when SD operations are properly planned and the area is mapped out in advance, the SD contingency should have the "home field advantage." We already know where the target's vulnerabilities are and we know where all the surveillance vantage points are. This means we can just pop in and out of the picture (preferably *behind* the surveillance vantage points) and avoid the risk of following anyone.

Remember that we, as SD operators, want to stay outside the

surveillance "Red Zone"—to see and remain unseen.

CHOOSING AN SD VANTAGE POINT

This one happens to quite a few SD operators. You find a nice spot at a comfortable distance where you can maintain visual control over things. All looks great until, oops—you realize you've actually put yourself in a good *surveillance* vantage point rather than an *SD* vantage point. Surveillance vantage points are where *surveillants* want to be, not SD operators. If we want to covertly detect hostile surveillants, then we would be wise not to sit right on top of them. Instead, as an SD operator, you'd want to position yourself where you can detect surveillants without them detecting you (which often means you'd want to be somewhere behind them).

Considering the fact that there's already a fair amount of distance between a good surveillance vantage point and the target, a good SD vantage point (which is behind the surveillance vantage point) is often quite far away from the client we're helping to protect. This can be a bit uncomfortable for security-minded operators, especially since this allows a potential enemy to be closer to your client than you are. Here, too, SD operators need to remind themselves that they're *not* responsible for immediate physical protection. Instead, you're providing an important function of field intelligence, so you can calm down about the distance factor.

MISTAKES AND LOUSY VANTAGE POINTS

Here you are, a well-trained SD operator, and all of a sudden you realize you just put yourself in a lousy SD vantage point—or find yourself enacting a classic mistake you were taught to avoid. Welcome to the real world of operational SD.

Now, should you be happy about making a blunder? Of course not. But should you abort the entire mission after realizing you've just made a mistake? No, not usually. There might be cases where a small misstep can indeed jeopardize an entire mission, or thoroughly expose you as an SD operator, but in most operations, this will not be the case. You'll just need to move on, avoid appearing nervous about the mistake you made (to prevent making it even worse), and try not to make the same slip-up in the future.

One good thing you have going for you is that it's very unlikely you'll get discovered as an SD operator, even after you've made a mistake. The few people out there who aren't consumed by their cell phones are usually consumed by other distractions, and they're miles away from noticing any mistakes—let alone concluding that someone's an SD operator.

Try to avoid mistakes, but don't panic when they inevitably happen.

This chapter covered several best practices for SD operations and talked about how to handle mistakes in the field.

In case you were wondering about some of the more common mistakes that covert operators make, and the general do's and don'ts of covert operations in general, you're in luck. The next chapter will cover a wide and colorful range of tips and insights into covert operations.

CHAPTER 9

LESSONS FROM THE FIELD: COVERT OPERATIONS

A technology conference somewhere in the Silicon Valley, 2013.

The tech conference was coming along well, and thousands of attendees were busily going in and out of the convention center during their lunch break. I was on my third day working undercover and was becoming quite familiar with the comings and goings of the area around the convention center.

It was then that I saw a casually dressed man in his mid-20s walk up to a newspaper stand, lean over on it and observe the main entrance to the convention center. It seemed pretty obvious to me that the guy wasn't actually a hostile surveillant. He was instead a member of the event security team—one who was trying (quite unsuccessfully) to take a covert position outside the venue. This young operator wasn't aware of me and my team being out there, and, with his appearance and behavior, he made a perfect display of almost all the classic covert methodology mistakes I teach my trainees and team members to avoid.

I'm not sure if he took it upon himself to provide this "covert" coverage, but after I reported his activities to our point of contact, he was promptly pulled out of the field and no other member of his protective team tried anything like that afterwards.

UNDERSTANDING COVERT OPERATIONS

One of the things that can happen when you get into the field of covert operations is that you start noticing more people working covertly, both on and off the job.

There's no surprise when this happens on the job (like in the case above), but the downside of having an eye for covert operations is that it's difficult to turn it off even when you're *not* on the job.

This means that, say, a stroll through an airport becomes a game of "find the covert security operators," and walking past a large protest (there are quite a few in the San Francisco Bay Area) becomes a game of "find the undercover cops." Once you know what to look for, games like these are not all that hard. I suppose it would be nice to just tune out this noise during my off-time and not play these games, but since I'm going to keep noticing all of this whether I want to or not, I decided long ago that rather than suffer from my involuntary hyperawareness, I might as well have a bit of fun with it.

To be clear, I do try to stay out of other people's business, and I never purposely go out of my way to look for covert operators. But, like it or not, if I can't help noticing things like the young, short-haired guys with untucked shirts and earpieces wheeling their empty hand luggage up and down airport terminals, then why not just embrace such things and make all that airport waiting time a bit more interesting?

Over the years, I've noticed a number of common difficulties and mistakes that covert operators tend to make. Needless to say, I too have made all of the blunders I examine in this chapter, and it's with this in mind that I offer my humble opinions, tips, and suggestions on the matter.

The following insights apply to most types of covert operations—from surveillance and surveillance detection to undercover investigations and covert security.

COVER AND COVER STORY

Let's start with the basics. A *cover* is the visual projection of what an operator wants people to see and therefore think of them. For example, if you want people to think you're a homeless person, you dress and look the part.

However, many operators make the mistake of formulating a cover that appears harmless, while forgetting that a cover that's interesting, fun, or attractive—like, say, a brightly dressed tourist—is almost always a bad one. It's bad because it fails the boring test. If there's anything memorable about the way you appear, then your cover is less than ideal.

A *cover story*, as its name implies, is the verbal representation of your cover. In other words, it's the story you tell, or the answer you give, if you find that you need to verbally explain who you are or what you're doing. For obvious reasons, your cover story has to fit and even strengthen your cover. Otherwise, it'll seem suspicious or curious if the person who looks homeless, for example, talks like a law enforcement officer.

One of the keys to the cover and cover story dynamic is to always start with a good cover and then work your way towards a supporting cover story. This order is important because the main idea is to visually embed yourself into the environment in such a bland and boring way that no one ever pays any attention to you, much less tries to question or talk to you. In an ideal situation, you would never even get to a point where you'd have to use your cover story.

As for the cover story itself, keep it simple and try to keep it within the boundaries of things you actually know from experience (so you can talk about it naturally and even elaborate if—and only if—you are asked to). At the same time, you want to stay far enough away from information that can lead back to who you really are. Do not volunteer too many details, and keep it bland and boring so that the person you're talking to will forget you as soon as they walk away.

POSTURE AND MOVEMENT

There's a celebrated quote by Winston Churchill, who, after being asked to what he attributed his success in life, answered, "Economy of effort. Never stand up when you can sit down, and never sit down when you can lie down."

This little tongue-in-cheek answer actually makes a good point when applied to covert operations. In most cases, movement attracts more attention than stillness, and standing attracts more attention than sitting. Bland and lazy are your best friends here.

In my experience, most people who gravitate towards covert operations tend to have backgrounds in military, law enforcement, or security—and sometimes all three. The reason I mention this is because people with these types of backgrounds naturally move and posture themselves in ways that are the opposite of bland and lazy. For the exact same reason that standing and moving around are good military, law enforcement, and security habits (allowing the operator to project more of a deterring presence while extending visual control), these same habits are bad for covert operations. The tendency to maintain a command presence and visually control your environment will usually make you stick out, as will any sudden movements, abrupt stops, or quick head turns. At the very least, these actions will make you look interesting, suggesting that there's something going on.

As a covert operator, you want to do the exact opposite and appear bland, lazy, and boring. Keep in mind that it will be difficult to pull this off if you're not actually comfortable. A person that's physically uncomfortable probably looks uncomfortable, and looking uncomfortable can attract interest, curiosity, and suspicion.

So relax, settle in, and try to get comfortable—which leads us to our next point.

SITTING DOWN

When you're on a covert surveillance or surveillance detection mission, it's almost always a good idea to sit down. The two main advantages that sitting down will give you are a less noticeable appearance, and the ability to see and notice more yourself. Though this seems like something the segment above already covered, I can't tell you how many times I've heard myself repeat the "Sit down!" instruction during trainings, and even during operations (which is why it deserves its own little segment).

Despite what you may see in Hollywood movies, there are relatively few reasons for being in a fixed position without sitting down. So once again, relax, settle in, *sit down*, and try to get comfortable.

NO CHANGING FIXED POSITIONS

So you sat down, great. Now stay there!

It's often the case that only *after* you've sat down at a vantage point that you notice an even better vantage point you could have picked. There's nothing ironic about this—you'll always be able to see and understand more after you stop moving and sit down (which is one of the main reasons you sit down in the first place). But as tempting as it is to move to that other, better position, it's often a bad idea.

There might be many legitimate, non-suspicious reasons for normal people to move from one nearby spot to another, but even in the best case scenario, doing this will make you stick out more than if you just stayed at your original spot. And remember, you are *not* a normal person—you're a covert operator moving from one vantage point to a better one (which is a classic surveillance indicator you'd want to avoid).

You've made your bed, now lie in it. Next time, try to find the better vantage point to begin with, but for now—stay put.

Surveillance Zone

THE BUS STOP

This one comes up a lot. You get to a new streetside location and quickly look for a good vantage point. As is often the case in urban areas, a bus stop just happens to be perfectly located for this. It often even has a number of people standing and sitting there—all the better for you to blend in. Good vantage point, right?

Wrong! Or at least almost always wrong (there are some exceptions, as usual).

Bus stops do indeed provide a logical justification for standing (or hopefully sitting) in very central locations, but this justification only makes sense if the bus stop is used for its intended purpose—to get on a bus. Using this vantage point for an extended period of time will not make sense because everyone else at the bus stop will eventually get on a bus, leaving the covert operator looking out of place. You might be able to justify a good 20-30 minutes at a bus stop, but eventually, you will have to board one of the buses that stops there.

Conversely, if you're conducting mobile surveillance and only need to buy yourself some 30-40 static seconds till you get moving again, a bus stop might seem very inviting. But this too isn't a great idea. Either spending too much time at a bus stop or quickly walking away from one without boarding a bus can get you detected.

Finally, if you absolutely *must* use a bus stop, pay attention to where the bus is coming from. The other people at the bus stop will almost always look that way, and you don't want to be the single person looking the wrong way.

CELL PHONES

Your cell phone can be your best friend or your worst enemy depending on how you use it. Not only is your cell phone the most natural and least suspicious way to communicate in general, but with the advent of smartphones, it can provide a necessary preoccupation that can justify your presence at various locations.

It might seem counter-intuitive for people on important covert operations to keep playing with their phones, but that's part of the point—appearing bored, distracted, and unprofessional is perfect for covering up what you're actually doing.

Look around you the next time you're out and about, and notice what bored and boring people are doing (remember, you want to look boring). Nine times out of ten they will have their smartphone in their hands. Additionally, your phone can even help you when conducting mobile surveillance on foot. As I mentioned earlier, unexpected stops are almost inevitable, and using your phone as a momentary justification for stopping (to seemingly answer some text message, for example) can be helpful at times.

One thing to keep in mind is that if you're going to use your phone to justify your presence or rationalize a quick stop, make sure you're actually doing something with it. In other words, don't just pretend to play with a blank screen.

It's also a good idea to silence your ringer. Although a ringing cell phone is not out of place, it can still draw attention to you. Likewise, if you're pretending to talk on the phone in order to justify your presence somewhere, you don't want your cell phone to start ringing while you're holding it to your ear (if someone actually calls you by chance). In addition to looking absurd, it can draw even more attention your way.

As for actually using the phone (or any device that looks like a cell phone) for verbal communication, always avoid using tactical language and try to remember that people on the street can hear what you're saying. Inexperienced operators have a bad tendency to say things like "Command from mobile-1. Target is traveling southbound on Franklin street."

Needless to say, this is not how most people talk on their phones. Rather than using call-signs, try using names (they obviously don't have to be your real names), and make up a name for your target, too—maybe something like Tim. So instead of the example above, why not say something like, "Hey Chris, it's Matt. What's up, man? I think Tim's actually heading down Franklin."

Also, keep in mind that most people don't call someone to say only one sentence, so you might want to keep talking. You don't have to fill up your communications network with chatter to do this—simply hang up (or cut off your audio) and blab on for a bit longer to make it seem more like a normal phone call.

If two operators are communicating with each other while in the same area (for example, inside a coffee shop or sitting on different benches in a city square), try not to start and stop communications at the same time since this can be detected as a correlation between the two operators. Instead, one of the operators should keep talking for a while after the other has gotten off the phone in order to make it seem like there is no connection between them.

As for hands-free extensions (both wired and wireless), I'm not a huge fan. For starters, unlike what you see in Hollywood movies, there's nothing all that covert about the classic radio surveillance kits that dangle a "pigtail" from your ear and force you to talk into your sleeve or collar (Secret Service-style). More advanced wireless skin-colored mini earpieces and microphones might do a better job of concealing themselves, but you'll still have to awkwardly (and suspiciously) talk into what looks like thin air. Of course, you could mask this by pretending to talk into a regular cell phone, but in that case, why not just talk into one for real?

The irony of using advanced technology for covert operations is that if these expensive tools ever get discovered, there's a much greater chance you'll get exposed than if you just text or call with an ordinary (or ordinary-looking) cell phone.

WORKING WITH OTHERS

When most people imagine what a covert operator looks like, they tend to think of a solitary individual (usually male). When instructing an SD course, I've found that it usually takes the trainees a few days to realize that it can be beneficial to work in pairs—or even groups—and indeed it is.

Few things are more innocuous looking than a man and woman sitting together in a coffee shop or walking down the street. What are the man and the woman doing over there? They're sitting and talking, right?

Yet another advantage that working in pairs can provide is teamwork. For example, two people can sit facing each other pretending to have a casual conversation while one is focusing on the target and describing what they see and the other (who's facing away from the target) jots down or communicates the information.

The main thing you want to avoid while working in pairs however is any type of meeting or splitting up in the field. If you come alone, you leave alone, and if you come together, you leave together. Watching people meet up or split up is much more memorable than seeing people arrive together and leave together. The absolute worst thing you could do—a classic mistake I've detected in real life—is to arrive in the area together and then split up to take different positions.

COFFEE SHOPS

You've probably noticed how often coffee shops come up when I discuss covert operations. This is because coffee shops provide some of the best vantage points (and are often located in areas where covert operations take place). Part of what makes coffee shops so ideal for surveillance and SD is that, unlike most other businesses, they will let you spend pretty much all day there, more or less unharassed. The closest thing to a coffee shop situation might be a restaurant, but those usually have servers who will keep checking on you and who will eventually expect you to pay for your meal and go on your way.

On a side note, if you must take position in a restaurant (maybe in order to closely surveil a hostile target or to covertly protect a client who's having a meal there), it's a good idea to pay for your meal as soon as it arrives. You won't want to frantically wave over your server for the check if your target or client begins to leave unexpectedly. Conversely—from the SD perspective—look out for restaurant patrons who pay for their meals as soon as they get them.

DEMOGRAPHICS

There's no point in ignoring this fact—the archetypal covert operator is male, somewhere between his 20s and 50s, and usually has a background in military, government, law enforcement, or security.

Lest you think this discriminates against those who don't fall into this demographic, let me assure you that the opposite is the case. Simply being female gives an operator a natural advantage, as does a younger or elderly appearance.

I can tell you from years of experience that some of the hardest individuals to detect (on both sides of the surveillance/SD fence) are quintessential "little old ladies," young Asian females, and anyone else who doesn't fit the mold that most people imagine when they think of a covert operator. The fact that you probably don't visualize people like this when the term "covert operator" comes up, and the fact that you'll rarely see them depicted in movies or on TV shows, is precisely the point. It's why these operators are so effective at remaining unnoticed.

PERSONALITY TRAITS

One of the most important, yet difficult, factors for covert operators to deal with is their personality—specifically, how it affects the way they appear to others. As I've mentioned before, people who gravitate towards covert operations very often have backgrounds in military, law enforcement, or security, and many operators with this type of experience tend to unknowingly reveal themselves in subtle ways—thereby harming their covers.

When considering how to dress for a covert operation, many people reach for the clothes they're used to wearing in their own real-life casual situations. The problem is that "casual" is a subjective idea that stems from (and therefore represents) your personality. And the personality of someone who's dedicated enough to get into covert operations isn't something you want to represent in your external appearance.

A common manifestation of this "casual" problem is the classic off-duty or low-profile agent look. It consists of jeans or cargoes, loose-fitting, untucked golf shirts or casual buttoned-up shirts (the kind that're good for concealing a weapon) and sporty or otherwise comfortable walking shoes. This look is common among people who want to be casual but also want to feel comfortable enough to jump into action if things "go south."

A few more easy giveaways I've seen over the years are tactical or sporty sunglasses (oftentimes Oakley's), tactical shoes and backpacks (most notably 5.11s), G-Shock type watches, tactical-looking ruggedized cell phone cases, clip-on pocket knives, golf or polo shirts worn over undershirts (oftentimes the Under Armour brand), baseball caps, soft-shell jackets, and anything that's considered "casual tactical" or "covert tactical." The supposedly covert operator I mentioned at the beginning of this chapter had pretty much all of these things on him.

Am I saying that anyone who possesses these items is necessarily a covert operator? Not at all. In fact, I can safely say that the vast majority of people sporting this stuff are nothing of the sort. But as a covert operator, wearing any of these items can increase your risk of being detected as a *potential* operator. And if you also happen to have a somewhat serious disposition, and you're occupying potential vantage points for long periods of time, you can get yourself detected as a *definite* operator.

I'll be honest, the typical low-profile agent look is one that I like myself, but the fact that someone with my background and personality likes it is all the more reason to avoid it when working in the field. A good way to go about selecting what to put on is to consider whether you think something looks good on you. Odds are if you think it looks good, it's probably because it fits and represents your personality, which means you should probably go change.

In the previous chapter, I talked about the benefits of the business-casual look. This advice can apply to other covert operations as well—depending on your cover and mission. But let's expand a bit more on the idea of purposely *not* looking the part and wearing something that *doesn't* represent who you are.

Most people have some articles of clothing in their house that they don't like—how about that pair of fashion jeans that your significant other got you a while back? Or how about that silly-looking cardigan sweater that some well-meaning aunt got you for Christmas a few years ago? The fact that these clothes don't suit your taste, and don't suit your idea of what might look good for a tactical operation, is precisely why they will do such a good job of masking who you really are and what you're doing.

This same principle also applies to your behavior, which we talked about earlier in the chapter. Conducting yourself in a way that looks dull or even somewhat dimwitted, as you slump down in your seat and play with your cell phone, might feel like the opposite of what you're used to or what seems appropriate for important tactical operations. But, once again, that's precisely what makes it so good for masking who you are and what you're doing.

Now that we've covered lessons and tips for working covertly in the field—including ways you can better blend in and remain hidden in plain sight—let's turn our attention to how you can better detect if you yourself are being surveilled. In the chapter ahead, I'll share some strategies to help you maneuver around certain types of surveillance and fill you in on a few tactics for evading watchful eyes.

CHAPTER 10

SURVEILLANCE DETECTION ON YOURSELF

San Francisco, 2012. I was enjoying a nice lunch at an Italian restaurant on a sunny Saturday afternoon in the North Beach district. My day had started on Market Street and I was having fun walking through the bustling tourist attractions around Union Square and Chinatown. To the casual observer, there was nothing special going on that Saturday, but I had noticed that a man followed me out of the Westfield mall, and then a second man also started trailing me shortly after I stopped for coffee at the Westin St. Francis hotel. The two then proceeded to follow me the entire morning, and now they were in different static positions observing the entrance to the restaurant I was in.

It sounds bad, I know, but this was actually what I wanted. In fact, I was the one who had contracted the two men to follow me. They were role-playing the part of hostile surveillants for a surveillance detection (SD) course I was co-teaching, and I was role-playing their target. All around us were the SD trainees, maintaining a longer distance and trying (quite successfully) to detect whether I was being followed.

Role-playing a surveillance target as many times as I have really taught me how to detect surveillance on myself. Although the surveillance role-players were contracted by me, I didn't inform them of where I was going and I wasn't directing their movements. It was up to them to keep track of me in the downtown San Francisco crowds. We do it this way in order to make these exercises as realistic as possible—giving the trainees a taste of the real deal.

The difficulty for me (as a simultaneous instructor and target role-player) is that I need to covertly notice if the hostile surveillance role-players are still following me or if they've lost me somewhere along the way (which does happen sometimes). If I fail to keep track of them, the exercises can flop (since the SD trainees won't have anyone to detect). However, if I don't keep track of things covertly (for example, if I constantly keep turning my head to look back), then the realism of the exercises will be harmed. Having done this for a good number of years, I've gotten to the point where I'm able to covertly detect the hostile surveillance role-players while also simultaneously keeping track of the SD trainees who are trying to detect them—all while this multi-layered dynamic is moving through busy downtown areas.

The neat thing about spending years getting proficient at something as strange and difficult as this is that when I get surveilled and followed in real life (which does occasionally happen), detecting these people turns out to be child's play.

HOW TO SPOT SURVEILLANCE ON YOURSELF

In this chapter, I introduce a number of techniques I've learned over the years to help you detect whether someone is surveilling you. But before we get started, I want to make it clear that my knowledge and experience comes from the private sector and not from any clandestine government agency work. Although the principles and techniques I'll be sharing here can be pretty effective across the board, I'm *not* trying to teach anyone how to detect government sector surveillance teams.

Because my own experience involves surveillance detection on foot rather than by vehicle, this will be our focus. The techniques I present here have been tested during training and successfully applied in actual, real-life situations.

So now that we've got that out of the way, let's get into it.

Where to Look

If you want to detect surveillance covertly (which doesn't always have to be the case, by the way), you'll want to avoid having your head on a swivel or constantly looking behind you. The best way to avoid these kinds of behaviors is by narrowing down the areas you'll be paying attention to and the types of behaviors you should be looking for. This type of narrowing down economizes your movements; thereby allowing you to detect things more discreetly.

The areas you'd want to pay attention to, and the things you'd want to look for, depend quite heavily on where you happen to be and on whether you're static or mobile. We've already covered most of the surveillance detection principles that apply in previous chapters, but in this chapter, the perspective we're taking is different. In this case, you're not looking for correlations to a third-person target—*you* are the target now.

With that in mind, let's consider where surveillance might be located so we can narrow down where to look for it.

Static surveillance:
If you're static, then there's a good chance that surveillance on you is also going to be static. Let's take the two most likely static locations

where someone might be able to find you—your home and your workplace. These are very important because, if you're being deliberately targeted, it's a safe bet to assume that you'll be found at these two locations on a regular or even routine basis, and it's not usually that difficult to find out where someone lives and works.

In order to figure out where surveillance might be, you'll want to put yourself in the shoes of a potential surveillant and try to figure out where you would locate yourself to covertly observe, say, the front door or driveway to your residence and the main entrance or parking lot entrance to your workplace. Don't just theorize about this, go ahead and actually try it out in the field. If you're a bit hazy on how to do this, revisit Chapter 4 where I discuss hostile surveillance in depth.

Are there any conveniently located cafés, busy intersections, bus or train stations, park or city benches, and the like that can give someone both a good view of your location and sufficient cover for an extended period of time? If so, those are probably the locations you'd want to focus your attention on.

You'd also want to pay attention to the vehicles that are parked in spots that could potentially give the surveillant a good view (which is especially important if the area doesn't have any good vantage points like the ones I just mentioned).

Mobile surveillance:
Now, if you're mobile, things become a bit more interesting since surveillance on you might also need to go mobile. When in motion, the surveillant will usually want to be somewhere behind you, and possibly behind and to the side. As you move forward on a typical city sidewalk, we can imagine potential surveillance "Red Zones" (one behind you and one behind but on the opposite side of the street) that will be "dragged" behind you as you move forward. This is something we discussed at length in Chapter 7.

One of the most challenging things for a mobile surveillant is what to do when you (the target) inevitably stop (either for a short or long period of time). This is because the dynamics switch from mobile to static and then probably back to mobile again. These transitional points present a real challenge for a surveillant—and, therefore, a detection opportunity for you—since the surveillant has to quickly and unexpectedly figure out how to keep track of you without displaying any signs of surprise, confusion, or nervousness. I go into detail about this in Chapters 6 and 7, but the difference here, once again, is that you're detecting surveillance on *yourself* rather than on someone else.

Now that we've figured out where to start looking, let's turn our attention to what you should be looking for, and how to look for it, while hiding the fact that you're trying to spot surveillance.

What to Look for and How to Look for It

As we've discussed at length in previous chapters, surveillance is primarily detected by noticing correlations to the target. The difficult part is detecting these correlations *covertly*, especially considering that the surveillant is most likely behind you or at angles that are purposely outside of your field of vision.

If you don't want to reveal the fact that you're looking for surveillance, you're going to have to find ways to briefly glance at these surveillance "Red Zones" and vantage points (both the static and mobile ones) in order to detect if the same individual might be correlating to you in observation, movement, various gestures, or mere presence. In other words, can you see if someone is looking at you, moving and stopping when you move and stop, preparing to leave when you're preparing to leave, nervously shuffling around when you come to a stop, or simply present somehow in different locations you happen to be in over time?

What distinguishes a surveillant from any other person out there is their *deliberate and consistent* attempt to observe where you are and where you're going. Therefore, the active correlations to you that a surveillant would have to exhibit—especially over time and distance—are the most important indicators that can set surveillants apart from the rest of the people around you. It's not always easy to spot these correlations, but, with practice, you can definitely get better at it.

The following techniques are designed to detect some of the classic indicators of surveillance. Keep in mind that this will probably not work if surveillance is conducted on a very high, government sector level or if you're being surveilled by a coordinated team of operatives.

The good news is that you can practice these techniques anytime and anywhere you want while gradually getting better and more subtle at applying them.

Static surveillance detection:

1. When you're at home, your place of work, a restaurant, a bar, and so on, try to find ways to look outside (for example, through windows or entrances) and see if you can spot anyone in a vantage point (or just lingering outside) who's paying close attention to the entrance.

2. As you exit, use natural head movements and peripheral vision to cover the vantage points. See if anyone takes note of your exit and if they're transitioning, or preparing to transition, from static to mobile—thereby correlating to your own transition.

Mobile surveillance detection:

1. As you move forward, try to find creative ways to take short glances at the area behind you and behind but on the other side of the street (the aforementioned Red Zones). A good way to do this is by periodically glancing sideways (for example, at stores,

cars, or people) and using peripheral vision to look behind you. In order to better hide the fact that you're doing this, try to make it visually obvious that you're interested in what's next to you rather than in what's behind you. Pick interesting-looking things to seemingly pay attention to (an attractive person, a flashy car, a unique store, etc.), but try not to exaggerate your movements or look sideways too much. Keep it nice and natural. All you need are short glances from time to time.

2. Use crosswalks, traffic lights, or other common reasons for short stops to naturally look around and therefore get an even better peripheral view of what's behind you. Here, too, keep it subtle and natural. You don't want to look directly backwards, and you don't want to make any nervous or abrupt head movements.

3. Find legitimate-looking reasons to cross to the other side of the street you're walking on. The 90-degree turn you'll be making puts the area that was behind you on your side now, which you can more easily and subtly cover with peripheral vision when you cross the street or wait to cross. This can also give you a subtle and logically justified head-on view of the other side of the street (which also contains a Red Zone you'd want to keep track of).

4. Use short stops (for example, to look at store windows, wait for a walk signal, or check your phone) and try to notice if anyone behind you has also abruptly transitioned from mobile to static (thereby correlating to your movements).

5. Use longer stops (like walking into a store, restaurant, or café) to quickly look out the front window or door and see if anyone

outside transitions from mobile to static. If anyone is observing the location you just walked into as they walk past in the direction you were going, or if anyone walks in after you, take note of them. Then repeat the two steps mentioned earlier regarding static surveillance detection. It's best to look ahead for good spots where you can do this. A store with a big window, for example, can serve this purpose. Make sure there's something of interest in front of that window to justify walking into the store and then seemingly looking at what's on display (while actually looking through the window to see the street). You can also use restaurants for this purpose, which often have menus posted next to the door, so you can pretend to read the menu as you use peripheral vision to look around.

6. Use little fakes to see if you can expose—and then detect—surveillance indicators. Keep it simple and subtle, but try doing things like the following:

   ▶ Walk past a store with a window front, then stop, turn around, and go back into the store.

   ▶ Gather up your things when you're sitting at a café and get up as if you're ready to leave, but then go and order something at the counter—or go to the restroom before returning to your table or to a different table.

There are many other similar actions you can perform, and techniques like these give you a chance to spot correlations by presenting your surveillants with potential stumbling blocks.

While the static and mobile SD tips I've shared in this section vary based on your circumstances, the point of all of them is the same—to help you covertly keep track of your surroundings and spot surveillants. A surveillant will always correlate to their target. The question is how well they'll be able to hide it, and actions like these can help you flush correlations out into the open.

Tricky Tricks

Many people like the Hollywood-type idea of using reflective surfaces, peepholes, or gadgets to either surveil others or spot if they're being surveilled themselves. I'm not a fan of this. I'm not saying that it's impossible to spot someone behind you by looking at a reflective surface, but you probably won't do well if you over-depend on such tactics.

Also, staring into a window (or rather at what it's reflecting) or using a blank screen of a laptop or cell phone to reflect what's behind you is more noticeable than you might think. The same problem occurs when you go for cliché moves like purposely dropping something in order to look around when picking it up, or stopping to tie shoelaces (that are already tied). I'm not saying these tricky tricks can never be useful or that they'll always backfire, just that they're riskier than you think, not likely to produce desirable results most of the time, and therefore not usually worthwhile. Basic, natural movements and behaviors are almost always the way to go instead.

Surveillance Detection Route

A surveillance detection route (SDR) is a predetermined route you can lure a surveillant into which is designed to subtly detect hostile surveillance. It basically incorporates all the abovementioned tactics into one planned sequence so that you can be less dependent on improvised, on-the-fly actions and more easily and covertly detect surveillance. SDRs can be used both on yourself or on others (for example, in the mobile surveillance situations I discussed in Chapter 7).

A typical route needs to start at a logical location where you are expected to be found (your workplace is a good one). The route should not be one that you ordinarily take because, if your surveillant already knows where you're going, they won't need to follow you (they could just wait for you there). Conversely, don't make this route too strange or tricky because the surveillant might not be tempted to follow you, or worse, might suspect that it's a trap.

Make sure the route has both short and long stops at predetermined locations where you already know what to look for and where to look from. These locations should be strategically chosen to allow you, with the right timing, to take glances at the surveillance Red Zones without it being apparent.

So now that we've covered how to spot surveillance, let's take a look at ways you can evade it if that's what you want to do.

SURVEILLANCE EVASION
Downtown San Francisco, 2011.
I was walking up Market Street wearing a blue buttoned-up shirt and a dark backpack. I made sure to keep a slow pace and to position myself in the middle of the wide sidewalk in order to make it easier for my pursuers to follow me from a distance. The idea was to be very noticeable and predictable and to lull the surveillants behind me—all five of them—into a comfortable, or even somewhat complacent, distance and pace.

When I eventually got to a BART station (the subway system in the San Francisco Bay Area), I quickly went down the stairs and turned the corner. At that point, I was fairly certain that no surveillant had eyes on me—at least for a few seconds until someone could get down there. While walking very fast in the station, I quickly took off my blue shirt (which I started unbuttoning as I went down the stairs), shoved it into my backpack, and put on a black baseball cap that I had in there. I then quickly popped out of an exit on the opposite side of Market Street and took off down a side street.

As my surveillants were struggling to reacquire the man wearing the blue buttoned-up shirt and dark backpack (who was walking at a slow pace westward on Market street) they didn't notice the guy in the white T-shirt and black baseball cap (holding his backpack with one hand down at his side), who popped out on the opposite side of the street and quickly disappeared onto Montgomery street.

Within seconds, nearly every single variable my surveillants were looking for had changed without them noticing. In the mix of a busy subway station and crowded intersection full of people and other distractions, their target had simply vanished. I know how shocked they were when it happened because they told me as much afterwards.

As you might have guessed, my surveillants were actually trainees at the end of a weeklong surveillance detection course. Now you might think that since this was just a training course that it would be much easier to pull this kind of thing off than if it were a real-life attempt to surveil me. But having experienced both situations numerous times, let me assure you that the opposite is the case. Unlike the actual surveillants I've had to shake off over the years (who were pretty amateurish), in this case, I had five very dedicated surveillants—most of whom had years of special forces, law enforcement, and security experience. All of them were doing their best to follow me, and at least one of them was barely ten seconds behind me on the street.

With this example of surveillance evasion fresh in your mind, let's take a look at various ways you can protect yourself from hostile surveillants.

Outmaneuvering the Hostile Surveillants

The first thing to understand here is that hostile surveillance isn't in and of itself the top threat you should be worried about. Surveillance is no more than an information collection tool; it's what this information is used for that should be of most concern. Evading surveillance, or otherwise protecting yourself from it, is therefore a way to protect yourself from a hostile tool—not the hostile goal—and this is an important distinction to keep in mind as we go along. Try not to make more out of hostile surveillance than it is, and try not to make more out of surveillance evasion than it is.

My knowledge on this subject comes from years of private sector security operations, where I trained in maneuvering around hostile surveillants and used various evasion tactics in real-life situations. Most of these real-life situations are cases where surveillants would try to follow me after I had finished leading a protective detail—mostly in San Francisco.

This kind of thing isn't always as ominous as it may sound (at least not to me). Various groups and activists that oppose political and corporate clients I've worked for sometimes just want to figure out who their security operators are. It is, nevertheless, something I don't much care for and something I've had to evade from time to time.

The good news is that surveillance is a pretty tricky business, which means that unless you're dealing with a very skilled and dedicated operative, or a team of operatives, it doesn't usually take much to shake off your surveillant. (I would sometimes even get a bit disappointed at how easy it was to elude most of them.)

Okay, so now that we've gotten that out of the way, let's look at a few strategies you can employ to protect yourself from hostile surveillance. We're going to start with some of the more basic, common sense approaches (which are actually very effective) and then make our way towards the sexier stuff—which I know you want to get to.

Surveillance Prevention

It's not necessarily possible 100% of the time, but one of the simplest ways to protect yourself from hostile surveillance is just to avoid it. This might sound strange, but you already know how to do much of this. Every time you avoid some dangerous part of town or decide not to walk down some dark alley at night, you're essentially avoiding the types of simple surveillance that precede most crimes. If you stick to safe areas and reduce your visual footprint, you'll reduce your risk of being targeted and followed in the first place.

Additionally, it's always best to keep a generally low profile when you go out and about. Luxury cars, expensive clothing, and flashy toys can make you stand out; as can acting out of place (like a tourist, a celebrity, a partygoer, and so on). You might be surprised to discover that many billionaire executives or otherwise influential individuals regularly walk around—carrying on a normal, largely unprotected lifestyle—by simply keeping a low profile. I can't say I'd necessarily recommend this (and have actually recommended otherwise to a good number of them), but I also can't deny the fact that they're usually not even noticed, let alone targeted by hostile surveillants.

With that said, here are a few simple measures (there are many more) that can help you prevent being surveilled. You can go as hard or as soft as you're comfortable with these—to each his own:

1. Try to vary your routines and routes of travel as much as you're comfortable with. Keep in mind that there will still be routines you won't be able to vary (like dropping off and picking up your kids from school or showing up to work on a regular basis), but there are little variables that can probably still be played with.

2. Try to exit through a different door than the one you entered. This will be easier in larger places like malls, hotels, and train stations. But you can also do this in many schools, offices, and apartment buildings (and even in some houses).

3. Try to avoid spending large amounts of time in static locations that can be easily surveilled from safe distances (street-side cafés and restaurants, parks, city squares, and so on).

4. When you meet up with someone, try to do so indoors (inside a café, a store, or a hotel lobby) rather than meeting on the street. Try not to wait outside places you're going to be spending time in.

Attrition

Most people might not realize this (since they haven't experienced how it feels to conduct surveillance), but spending hours and hours in one location might very well discourage a less committed surveillant from sticking around. Don't underestimate how tedious surveillance can be. Unless you're dealing with a real professional, or just an extremely dedicated opponent, you can simply bore surveillants off of you. It's the opposite of flashy, but it can be quite effective.

Run!

It's as simple as that. A faster moving target is harder to follow. You might think that running implies danger or emergency, but it's not all that uncommon to see people running down the street (for exercise, to catch a bus that's pulling up, to make it in time for a meeting, and so on). It doesn't have to be a frantic situation, and you don't have to run all that fast (you can even just walk really fast if you'd like), but if you're not particularly interested in covertly finding out who your pursuer is—or you're just interested in taking a precautionary measure—speeding up remains a decent option.

Movies and TV shows often depict this as ending very badly—getting yourself cornered in some dark alley—but this obviously doesn't have to be the case. Why not run into a crowded mall or hop onto a bus that's about to take off? It's basically the opposite of the attrition idea where you bore someone off of you. Here, too, unless you're dealing with a real professional, or just an extremely dedicated opponent, you can often outrun them or just make yourself a harder and less worthwhile target to pursue.

Deterring Measures

I often find that when the subject of hostile surveillance comes up, many people automatically take a "cloak and dagger" approach—trying to covertly detect, evade, or counter. This might be important in some scenarios, but there are also many cases where a conventional, overt approach can be even better.

For example, you can make it visually clear to everyone around you that you're aware of your environment and are therefore not an easy or desirable target. If you feel like someone's surveilling you, you can just start looking back at them. You can even follow this up by filming them on your cell phone. Depending on the situation (if it's safe to do so), you might even want to confront them, ask them who they are and what they want. Inform them that you're going to call the police (and then call the police if necessary) or otherwise show them that they've been completely "burned." You don't have to let them follow you home, to an important location, or to an area that might be less safe for you. Just because we tend to get caught up in the sexy intrigue of covert operations doesn't mean we should never consider conventional, common sense measures like these.

Lest you think this approach only applies to low-level situations, I know a former member of the Israeli Security Agency (often referred to as Shin Bet), who once took this approach when he was in charge of security at an Israeli embassy back in the early 90s (I won't specify which country this was in). Three agents from an enemy state used to regularly occupy a table at a restaurant that had a clear view of the embassy. They had long been detected, and at a certain point, when the Israelis grew tired of this, my friend took a large camera, walked into the restaurant, stood in front of their table, said hi, and snapped close-up photos of each of the men. He then bid them farewell and walked back to the embassy. The three were not seen back there again.

Evasive Maneuvers

Okay, so now we get to the sexier part you've been waiting for.

First, this might come as a surprise, but evasive maneuvers don't always have to follow surveillance detection. I know this sounds strange, but you can actually evade surveillants without knowing where they are or even if they exist. Whether you've detected a surveillant or not, you'll probably be getting rid of them in the same manner anyway, so there's usually no harm in just breaking out some evasive maneuvers.

These maneuvers might only take a few extra seconds or minutes to employ (a small price to pay even if it just turns out to be a precautionary measure). It would obviously be nice to detect whether you're actually being surveilled, but without a good amount of training and experience (and oftentimes even with it), this can be a difficult and time-consuming task. So why wait if you're just going to be taking the same evasive actions anyway?

The key to understanding evasive maneuvers is to first get acquainted with how surveillance works—to understand its difficulties and exploit its vulnerabilities. We've talked about this at length in previous chapters, particularly in Chapters 4 through 7, but the opportunities you're looking to exploit are the brief periods when your surveillant will not be looking directly at you.

These inevitable moments will almost always occur when you're mobile since the surveillant will also have to look where they're going, maintain a bit of distance, let their target go around a corner first before following it, and so forth. The vulnerability you'll be exploiting here is the surveillant's difficulty in keeping track of their target (especially in crowded areas)—something I illustrated at the start of this section. This leads the surveillant to latch onto certain visual cues (like appearance, pace, and direction of travel). This natural tendency to latch onto visible variables is what opens up the surveillant to deception by means of quickly changing those variables and breaking out of what they're expecting to see.

Here's what has worked for me:

1. Establish a slow, stable pace of movement that will be easy to surveil from a comfortable distance.

2. Find a spot somewhere ahead of you that allows you to break out of your surveillant's visual field—even if just for a few seconds. This could be as simple as turning a corner or walking into a department store, train station, or hotel lobby (advance knowledge of the area can take this to a higher level).

3. Use the brief interval—just after you've exited your surveillant's field of vision—to quickly change as many of your visual variables as you can (appearance, body language, pace, and direction of movement). That way, by the time your surveillant reaches a point where they expect to reacquire you (based on the appearance, body language, pace, and direction you've caused them to expect), none of those variables apply to you anymore.

The principles at play here aren't all that different from the ones professional illusionists use—lulling their audience into false expectations, redirecting their attention and making a simple sleight of hand trick look like a disappearing act. It's good to practice the technical aspects of this but don't forget that beyond the physical movements, like most good illusions, surveillance evasion is more of a psychological trick you play on your audience—one where the hostile surveillants are left scratching their heads after you somehow disappear.

Beyond the coolness factor of surveillance detection and evasion, the techniques covered in this chapter can be useful to a wide slice of the population. They don't just apply to covert operators who protect Silicon Valley CEOs. They're applicable to travelers, journalists, people who are being stalked, or anyone who's interested in raising their level of awareness, becoming more conscious of what's around them, and being proactive about their personal security.

CHAPTER 11

CIRCLES OF SECURITY

Shareholders meeting. Silicon Valley, 2010. When a large and controversial corporation holds a shareholders meeting, it's never as simple as booking a room and inviting attendees. Considerable resources are often invested in securing these events. To get an idea of just how important this is to some companies, consider the fact that the number of shareholders attending these small meetings (usually 50-100) is sometimes matched by the number of professionals who secure them. For this particular meeting, those working the event included law enforcement agents, campus security officers, corporate security operators, protective intelligence analysts, and outside contractors (like the team I was leading). My team alone had twelve operators.

Security for the event started at the street entrance to the corporate campus. As the shareholders made their way past that initial layer, they were met with more security screening at the parking lot, and then again at the walkway leading towards the venue. At the end of the walkway, we'd set up a bag check station (no bags, recording devices, or even cell phones were allowed into the meeting). And finally, before shareholders were allowed entrance, they needed to pass a full metal detection screening and close-up evaluation (which I was directly in charge of). Security inside the venue was also extensive, consisting of both overt and covert elements.

Most people might not realize this, but individuals from various activist groups and opposing organizations often manage to enter shareholders meetings like this. And no, it's not a lapse on the part of security; these individuals actually purchase shares in the corporations they oppose in order to become legitimate shareholders who can then attend these important meetings. This is one of the difficulties a company has to deal with when it becomes publicly traded—and therefore subject to all manner of federal Securities and Exchange Commission (SEC) stipulations regarding shareholders' rights. It's for this reason that attendees of an event like this have to go through multiple layers of screening.

Once screening for the meeting was well underway, I was notified by an operator at one of the outer security layers that a suspicious individual was making his way towards us. He had been politely engaged by security personnel and promptly responded by displaying his official invitation to the event. Still, his clothing, strange attaché bag, and body language indicated that something wasn't quite right.

By the time he got to the metal detectors, clutching a folder of flyers and papers he'd taken out of the bag he had to check, he was recognized as a member of an activist group that opposed the corporation. I made sure to direct him to a specific metal detector and proceeded to check him myself. Before crossing the magnetometer gate, he placed the few personal items he had on the designated tray for inspection. But I noticed he still had a pen in his shirt pocket, so I politely asked him to put it in the tray. Further noticing his strange behavior and reluctance to part with the pen before eventually putting it in the tray, I picked it up to inspect it more carefully. It was then that I realized this was no ordinary pen: it was a cleverly disguised pen-recorder that he was trying to smuggle into the meeting.

Needless to say, he was unsuccessful.

Even though the pen itself was small and mostly hidden, suspicious indicators about the individual carrying it were already noticed well in advance, and he was flagged for extra special screening before he ever made it to my access control station. Taking our time to screen him and his belongings more carefully, the pen recorder was actually quite easy to find.

WHAT ARE CIRCLES OF SECURITY?

In the field of security, we have a time-tested strategy known as *Circles of Security* that falls somewhere between conventional and unconventional protective operations. Essentially, what this involves is concentric layers of security screening around a protected asset or property. There are many different ways to employ Circles of Security, and, depending on resources and physical barriers, there is no real limit to the number of circles one can employ (in most cases, the more circles the better). Generally, you'll find that these security circles fall into one of three categories: the Inner Circle, the Outer Circle, and the Intelligence Circle.

The Inner Circle can be defined as the asset or property that's being protected, along with its immediate exterior. The Outer Circle is the whole area around the asset or property, stretching as far as a security officer can realistically visually control (between 1 and 3 blocks on average).

In addition to the Inner and Outer Circles, we have a third and much wider circle—the Intelligence Circle. This is the interesting juncture where you begin to expand outwards from direct physical protection and enter the realm of intelligence, which includes such things as online presence and remote information collection. This circle also has a field component (Field Protective Intelligence) which is where surveillance detection can mostly be found.

The relationship between these three circles is the subject of this chapter, so let's start by exploring the Outer Circle and then make our way from there.

THE OUTER CIRCLE

One of the ironies of employing this somewhat unconventional protective layer is that it's difficult for your average person to understand why it works. The Outer Circle does such a good job of preventing hostile attacks, and it does it so subtly and unobtrusively, that it creates a situation where many people don't even realize it's there.

In many ways, this is exactly what we're going for—prevention of hostile activity with minimal disruption to business and maximum customer service. The small tradeoff to this, however, is that some people may mistakenly conclude that nothing much is being done to protect them. Thankfully, this confusion can be dispelled by explaining how the Outer Circle works.

This starts by getting a notion of where crime, in general, and hostile attacks, in particular, come from. We do this by analyzing case studies and learning from the testimonies of captured attackers and hostile planners. What becomes quickly apparent is that hostile attacks don't just come out of nowhere, and hostile attackers don't simply materialize at their intended targets. Criminal activity is always preceded by some form of hostile planning, which is something we discussed in Chapter 4.

Usually, the bigger and more consequential the crime, the more planning that needs to go into it. Hostile planning is basically a decision-making process that begins by picking a specific target (out of a number of potential ones) and then nailing down the details of how, where, and when to attack it. In order to determine the best target, a hostile entity must first weigh the pros and cons of each potential target. One of the most consistent findings in case study research is that it's the easiest potential target that gets picked by the hostile entity (easiest in relative terms compared to the other potential targets). After this, the hostile entity will spend more time observing their selected target in order to collect more detailed information.

And this is where the Outer Circle comes into the picture. You can make a protected asset or property a less desirable target by employing three Outer Circle measures:

1. Deterrence by appearance
2. Detection
3. Exposing

Deterrence by appearance is designed to give a potential hostile observer enough visual information to dissuade them from choosing the property in question as the final target. To do this, security doesn't necessarily have to be aggressive or overly restrictive—solid security basics like the visual projection of presence and a high level of awareness, vigilance, and professionalism is usually enough.

In addition to deterrence by appearance, the Outer Circle continues by adding an active attempt to *detect, acknowledge,* or *expose* any person spending time in the area (regardless of whether or not they seem suspicious). This means that even if a hostile entity wasn't deterred by the appearance of professional security officers, the act of being observed, acknowledged, and sometimes even politely engaged by security officers will most definitely have a strong deterring effect—additionally raising the probability that the hostile entity will either abandon its plan or take it elsewhere.

What makes the Outer Circle so useful for facilities, campuses, and special events is its ability to deter hostile planning without compromising customer service or offending non-hostile individuals. (It's one of those rare cases where you can make an omelet without breaking any eggs.) This is because hostile planners observe a potential target with a very different mindset than that of an ordinary person. While looking for the easiest potential target and collecting pre-attack information on it, a hostile planner is extremely careful not to lose the element of surprise or get exposed. Hostile planners are therefore extremely aware of, and hypersensitive to, any attention they might receive—most notably from law enforcement or security.

It's natural for people to think of hostile attackers as callous and ruthless individuals, and this might be true enough when talking about the attack itself. But research and experience have shown that before the attack—during the hostile planning process—the opposite is the case, and hostile planners are much more cautious and sensitive than most people think. An attacker might not necessarily be afraid of getting harmed during the attack, but the planner (even if it's the same person) is absolutely afraid of getting acknowledged, exposed, or caught during the planning stage. A hostile planner is therefore very susceptible to any indication that a potential target might not be as good or easy as another, and this is exactly the vulnerability that the Outer Circle strategy seeks to exploit. It's not about scaring anyone away; it's about painting a less favorable picture for those looking for an easy target and making it more likely that they'll either abandon their plan or take it elsewhere.

The misconceptions that many people have about the Outer Circle strategy (that security isn't doing anything or that it's "security theater") usually have two root causes:

1. **It's hard to measure.** The irony in preventive security is that the more effective it is, the harder it is to measure its success (because nothing bad ever happens). It's akin to the modern misconception about the importance of vaccines, which have been so quietly effective at preventing and even eradicating dangerous diseases that many people no longer understand why they're so necessary.

2. **It's almost invisible.** The Outer Circle strategy is calibrated to target the specific vulnerabilities of hostile planners. Ordinary people—who have nothing to hide, harbor no hostile intentions, and are at no risk of exposure—have no reason to notice what is actually going on.

With that said, I never blame anyone for having these misconceptions. It simply means you're a decent, non-hostile individual—the kind of person this strategy is designed to welcome rather than deter. And the fact that regular folks have these misconceptions in the first place is actually a testament to how effective, yet non-intrusive, this strategy is.

So now that we understand the basics of the Outer Circle, let's take a look at how it works in the field.

Initial Screening of the Area and Establishing Visual Control

When you first take position in the Outer Circle, you'll want to spend a limited amount of time (measured in minutes usually) to screen and observe the area very closely. You'll need to do this in order to familiarize (or refamiliarize) yourself with the area in question. It's also important to establish visual control and maintain awareness, but this only comes *after* you've initially established that there's nothing suspicious in the area that's already waiting for you.

I define visual control as *the ability to visually keep track of an area of interest*. It's not so much that you're *physically controlling* the area, it's that you're maintaining *cognitive awareness* of what's going on in it; noticing people and keeping track of things as they change over time. Which leads us to our next section...

What to Look For

If you ask most people what they need to look for in the Outer Circle, they'll usually say "anything suspicious." (I know this for a fact after posing this question to hundreds, if not thousands, of operators for over a decade.) The problem with this thinking, however, is that the *anything* part of "anything suspicious" is way too vague and general. I'm absolutely interested in detecting anything suspicious on the property in question, but at a distance of a block, or a few blocks, what I'm most interested in is *people*.

Just like weapons and explosives don't deploy themselves, information doesn't collect itself, and hostile plans don't just plan themselves—it takes people to do these things, and that's why I'm primarily interested in people at these distances. It's true that cameras and recording devices can also be used for hostile planning and that these can be hidden in vehicles that are left in the area. But keep in mind that someone has to *bring* these devices here first; someone has to park the car and then return to retrieve it; someone needs to figure out where to point the camera or recording device in the first place. Gadgets and technology can certainly make it easier to plan and execute hostile activities, but they're not going to completely eliminate the human factor (at least not yet).

Now that we've screened the area and know what to look for, we need to devise a strategy for keeping track of everything, and this is where we come to the concept of zoning.

Zones

The same way it's difficult to navigate without a map, it's hard to secure an area that you don't understand. A good way to solve this is to take the large area you're trying to keep track of and break it up into well-defined zones. The zones obviously don't change the area itself, but they change the way you observe and think about it—making it easier to categorize, contextualize, and keep track of things. Think of this like chapters in a book or paragraphs on a page. It's the same number of words, they're just better segmented for easier comprehension and reference.

There are many ways to zone an area (for example, using numbers, letters, or codes), but the idea is the same. You take a large and mostly unfamiliar swath of city, break it up into segments, and give each segment what's essentially an address or zip code.

For example, it's a bit difficult to keep track of information about someone who's hanging out somewhere in the general vicinity. But as soon as you reframe this as an individual who's sitting in the middle of, say, Zone 2, it becomes a lot easier. There's an address for it now—Zone 2—which gives you a defined location. The better you've define an area, the easier it is to keep track of what's going on there, and breaking up a large area into zones is the best way to get this started.

After you've broken the area up into zones, the next step is to take a quick inventory of what's in each zone. Remember, we're mostly concentrating on the people who are spending time in each zone, but it's also important to keep track of things like vehicles.

The way this works is that you give a brief but descriptive nickname to every individual you see. I usually just base it on their appearance (for example, "Zone 2 brown sweater guy" or "Zone 3 old lady with a dog"). As for vehicles, you won't have to come up with nicknames for them because vehicles already have names (their make and model). Therefore, in Zone 2, you may have that "brown sweater guy" sitting on a bench and a Civic, Accord, Camry, and Corolla parked on the street.

Now, you're not actually trying to memorize all this information. You might have lots of people and cars in the area, and unless you have a photographic memory, storing all this information in your head while you're also performing other security functions would be way too much to expect.

Instead, what you're trying to work on here is *recognition*. This means you don't have to remember exactly what's in each zone, you just have to be able to recognize a person or vehicle if you see them again. If a few minutes have passed since you last looked at Zone 2, and now you see a man with a brown sweater (our "brown sweater guy") sitting on a bench—along with a Civic, Accord, Camry, and Corolla parked on the street—you should be able to recognize these things, and they should look familiar to you since they were all there the last time you looked. If, on the other hand, you now see a Ford F-150 in Zone 2, it's enough to realize that it doesn't look familiar to you since it wasn't there the last time you looked.

You're only human, and you won't be able to see every single change as it happens, but you will want to notice changes as soon as you can and without wasting too much energy. If you spot a change, there's usually no cause for alarm—cars and people come and go all day long. See if there's anything suspicious about the F-150, and if not, add it to the inventory you're keeping on Zone 2.

I know that the idea of zoning and taking inventory sounds like a huge undertaking, but it really only takes a few seconds to get it started. And once you've gone over your zones a few times, you'll be surprised at how quickly you can become familiar with an area you may have never been to before.

Also, keep in mind that the inventory you're taking is just for maintaining visual control. In other words, unless there's some kind of active incident, you don't need to report all the details you see out there. All you're trying to do is get to a level of familiarity that will make it easier for you to spot things and keep track of changes.

The hardest part in the visual control game isn't actually a visual issue, it's a concentration and focus issue. The problem isn't with your eyes, it's with your mind. Anyone who's not visually impaired can physically see people, the question is whether you can recognize and keep track of them.

Now that we've essentially covered our outfield (the Outer Circle), let's turn our attention to the infield and how to secure this important area.

THE INNER CIRCLE

The general idea of the Inner Circle (which usually applies to facilities and campuses) is to control the property in question in order to secure its assets. You'll want to start this process with an initial check of the property to make sure it's secure—usually by means of a security sweep. For special events or projects where the property is only leased temporarily, this initial check is extremely important. With permanently owned facilities and campuses (which can be controlled and monitored continuously), this initial check usually takes place during the opening procedures at the beginning of the morning shift.

After you've determined that you have a secure location, you'll want to maintain this security by making sure nothing harmful breaches it. This is generally achieved by limiting the number of entry points and controlling those that do remain open, which brings us to our next topic.

Access Control

This section deals with the human factor of access control—that is, the functions that security personnel provide. However, electronic measures can also fall into this category. For example, keycard readers, coded entrances, and intercom systems are all considered types of access control too.

When most people think about access control, they imagine themselves standing in front of a gatekeeper—perhaps a security guard or receptionist—where questions might be asked, credentials or appointments might be checked, and a follow-up sign-in process might be necessary. However simple or thorough the access control process might be, people usually focus on the Inner Circle part of it—where there are only a few feet between the screener and the individual who is being screened.

However, it's important to note that the process of assessing individuals and determining whether they should be granted access should not begin at such close quarters—it should end there. People don't simply materialize in the Inner Circle. They have to come from somewhere, and wherever they might be coming from, they must first—by definition—pass through the Outer Circle.

This is why, from a security perspective, it's useful to start by looking at the Outer Circle and work your way inwards. It is, after all, the path that any person wishing to enter must take—including would-be infiltrators. You always want to start the process of evaluating individuals as early as you can and from as great a distance as possible—the earlier and farther, the better.

The benefits of this are easily illustrated when considering worst-case scenarios. For example, if you have to deal with an armed attacker, you'll most certainly want to realize what's coming as early and as far away from the access point as possible. It might be too late for preventive measures, but the distance and time you'll have will help you in your emergency response. If you wait until the individual is right in front of you, it might be too late to do anything.

This means that the ideal location for access control is a vantage point where security officers can visually control the Outer Circle as well as a choke point where they can physically control the entrance. Obviously, this can be a bit tricky if the access control station must be inside the building. However, the ideal way to deal with this problem (if budgets allow) is to split the access control into two parts: an initial, outdoor area controlled by officers in charge of Outer Circle security and a secondary, indoor area controlled by the Inner Circle team. A good analogy for this is your classic air filter, which works by first filtering out any large debris (the Outer Circle) before sending the remaining particles to the finer, secondary filter (the Inner Circle).

Even if the above split isn't possible and access control can only be conducted indoors, in almost every case I know, facility entrances are made of glass. This gives officers the advantage of being able to see people before they enter. In order to facilitate this, make sure your access control station is facing that entrance rather than sitting at an angle to it. Even if this only buys you an extra few feet and an extra two seconds to observe people, it's better than completely relinquishing your observational skills until an individual is right on top of you.

OBSERVING TRANSITIONS FROM THE OUTER TO INNER CIRCLE

We've talked about how the Outer and Inner Circles work, but how do we evaluate individuals from a distance as they transition between these areas?

For example, let's say we're stationed in the Inner Circle and someone is approaching us from the Outer Circle. We're not close enough to notice little details or ask them any questions. However, what we *can* do is begin to assess them using two important indicators: their appearance and body language. The closer the person gets to us, the more features become visible, and the finer our filtration and evaluation abilities become. Essentially, we're using our powers of inductive observation here, which is something I discussed at length in Chapter 3.

When you're positioned correctly for this type of access control, you should be able to observe when and how people transition from the Outer Circle to the Inner Circle as they approach. Try to establish some general baselines for how people normally look and behave when they do this. Use your inductive observation skills to notice the general differences between people who:

- Spend time in the Outer Circle *without* approaching the Inner Circle

- Spend time in the Outer Circle *before* approaching the Inner Circle

- Walk right up to the Inner Circle *without spending any significant time* in the Outer Circle

Start noticing how people look and behave—both *before* and *during* their transition between the circles. For example, it's quite normal for people to arrive early for a meeting or a special event, spend some time in the Outer Circle, and then approach the Inner Circle. But try to also notice the appearance and behavior of people who deviate from norms like this.

From years of experience, I can tell you that most people who try to enter secured locations for illegitimate reasons don't take into account that security might be watching their transitions from the Outer Circle to the Inner Circle. My personal favorite example are flash-mob protesters because they're usually harmless, and because they provide a fun visual seminar on covert methodology mistakes.

These folks never seem to realize how obvious they are when they assemble or arrive together somewhere in the Outer Circle and then split up to try to nonchalantly enter the Inner Circle separately. Needless to say, most people don't act that way, and properly trained and positioned security officers should be able to spot such things.

If these people end up gaining access to the Inner Circle (which is not uncommon in more public locations like hotel lobbies, public squares, or open campuses), you'll notice how they take strategic positions once inside and how they exchange subtle nods and glances. Pay enough attention and you might also notice that many of them have the same kind of backpacks (usually containing banners) and that they often talk to each other on their cell phones, not realizing that someone with covert methodology training can easily spot this.

Controversial events like political rallies and some shareholders meetings often attract protesters, which—in keeping with constitutional rights—are usually allowed to assemble somewhere in the Outer Circle. (Typically, this is across the street or generally off the property.) Having managed security for dozens of events like this, I can tell you that it's not uncommon for some protesters to try to get into the venue in order to disrupt it or collect intelligence on it. Protesters sometimes even spend quite a bit of money on tickets, company stocks, donations, or whatever's necessary to acquire legitimate means of entry. For this reason, it's always important to position security operators to observe if any individuals transition from an Outer Circle protest to the Inner Circle venue, and to relay this information to the access control officers. This forward observation can be conducted either overtly or covertly, both having plusses and minuses depending on the situation and the desired effect.

LOOKING FOR SUSPICIOUS INDICATORS

When you're performing security, one of your key tasks is to keep an eye out for any suspicious indicators, but these aren't always obvious or easy to spot. For example, it's somewhat safe to assume that nonviolent, would-be infiltrators—the kind that are only interested in disrupting an event or secretly recording it—would be harder to detect than a would-be violent attacker. This is because the former would not necessarily exhibit the same type of fight-or-flight, Adrenalin-driven indicators that we might expect from the latter. However, the good news is that a well-trained team can detect both cases by making the most of the Inner and Outer Circle relationship.

Metal detector gates, which we often employ for controversial or high-threat events, provide a good example of how trained professionals can detect even the subtle indicators that are displayed by nonviolent yet disruptive individuals. By themselves, metal detectors only screen for metallic objects. They aren't actually going to pick up on leaflets or paper banners—much less subtle indicators like nervousness or evasiveness. Nevertheless, we're always assessing more than just an electromagnetic disturbance when deploying these devices.

Whenever possible, it's important to position forward observers ahead of the metal detectors. To the untrained eye, these officers are supposedly there for ushering and customer service purposes (smilingly assisting and directing people), but the underlying reason for them to be there is to observe people's reactions when they first realize there are metal detectors to go through. The key is to notice how people approach—how they look and behave when they transition from the Outer Circle to the Inner Circle and first realize that they're going to have to go through metal detectors.

An observant and well-positioned officer should be able to notice certain appearance and behavior features which can indicate that a person might not necessarily be interested in happily attending an event or meeting. The initial detection of this can usually be done from a distance, and by the time the person reaches the metal detectors at the access control station, officers can confirm it when they screen the individual more closely.

Having caught countless individuals trying to enter venues for illegitimate reasons, or sneak contraband in, I can say that once you know what to look for, detecting these individuals is not all that difficult. Too many people think security is all about gadgets or nifty tricks for detecting objects and miss the point about evaluating the person.

Now you might think that more infiltrators and disrupters (violent or nonviolent) would figure out a way to outsmart such a simple means of forward observation, detection, and information relay, but you would be mistaken. When I first started out in this line of work, I used to wonder why these people don't just dress and act normally to avoid being detected—like you often see in the movies. I'm not saying it's impossible for a skilled individual to completely evade security detection, but from years of field experience, I can tell you that it's very different from what you see in the movies. We do sometimes employ measures like surveillance detection in order to spot more skillful planners. But when dealing with most protestors, disruptors or illegitimate infiltrators, there simply are no James Bond types trying to do this kind of stuff, at least not in the private sector spheres I've been operating in.

As it turns out, personality, motivation, nervousness, and even ideology will almost always manifest themselves in some way. And these manifestations (even the subtle ones) can be picked up by skilled officers as long as they're positioned correctly, know what to look for, and in some cases, know how to elicit them.

ELICITING DETECTABLE INDICATORS

A common misconception about access control is that the flow of information is a one-way street—from the individual in question towards security. But there's no reason for security to take such a passive stance. Officers can actively send out non-verbal challenges to the people who approach the Inner Circle, and they can do so while the individuals are still in the Outer Circle.

I like to think of these little challenges as relatively easy "curveballs" that the officer throws at those approaching in order to see how they handle them. These challenges can be as simple as showing the individual that you've detected them with a polite nod of the head. To most non-hostile people, this doesn't mean much, and is therefore not a curveball that'll give them any trouble. It shouldn't offend them or cause them to react in any suspicious manner—maybe they nod back, maybe they don't—but in either case they'll just keep walking towards you normally.

However, to someone with hostile or disruptive intent—a person who still has something to hide while in the Outer Circle—being detected and acknowledged by security before they even reach the Inner Circle paints a pretty bad picture—one that's likely to evoke a nervous response. Even if this nervous response is subtle (for example a flinch, double-take, or slight change of walking speed), the timing of it, and the officer's training to look for it, should provide a sufficient reason for extra observation, scrutiny, and questioning when the individual reaches the Inner Circle. The idea here is to give individuals who already have a good reason to be nervous a reason to inadvertently display their nervousness—and do so from a distance.

Metal detectors, as I mentioned earlier, are another good example of this because they provide quite a curveball to throw at people who are not ready for them. This means that we don't want to miss their reactions when they first see them. It's natural for many people to be a bit surprised when unexpectedly seeing metal detectors at an entrance to a facility or venue. But there's a natural and normal type of surprised response, often accompanied by annoyance or uncomfortable laughter as the individual keeps approaching at the same speed and with roughly the same body language. And then there's a not-so-natural or normal type of surprised response, often accompanied by indicators of nervousness, change of walking speed, stopping, turning around, double takes, quickly checking pockets or bags, and so on. To miss these types of elicited responses is to miss a big part of what we're trying to screen for as people transition between the Outer and Inner Circle.

THE INTELLIGENCE CIRCLE

Remember the story I shared at the start of the chapter? The one about the pen recorder that I caught on an individual who was trying to sneak it into a shareholders meeting? Well, there was actually another layer to this story that began before this guy even made it to the event. Security for the shareholders meeting actually extended well beyond the Outer Circle and included an additional layer of protection I call the *Intelligence Circle*.

The Fortune 100 corporation we were working for placed (and still places) a great deal of importance on protective intelligence—and for very good reason. Before the event began, we had gained intelligence (mostly from social media sources) about specific individuals who were planning to get themselves into the meeting by legitimate means (acquiring share ownership and signing up for the meeting). Not only did we gain vital intelligence about their intentions, but we even knew how many of them would be coming and who they were.

However, having all this intelligence did not in any way diminish the need for, or the importance of, the Inner and Outer Circle relationship. In fact, based on their appearance and behavior alone, these individuals would have been flagged for extra scrutiny anyway. But the fact that we did have intelligence on them made our job easier and added an extra bit of pin-pointed accuracy that you usually don't get in conventional security operations. This accuracy applied to the extra thoroughness with which the access control officers screened these individuals, and extended into the various covert measures that were taken in the meeting itself (which I will not discuss here).

Another case where we received that kind of intelligence happened before a large political event we were protecting in the Silicon Valley back in 2008. The details we got were very precise and included the name and even the photo of an individual who belonged to a student organization that vehemently opposed our client. We even knew by what legitimate means the individual intended to enter. We advised our client not to let him into the event but were told that for public relations reasons, he was not to be turned away. We were instructed to screen him well but to allow him to enter.

An Open Source Intelligence (OSINT) investigation on the individual indicated there was a low-medium probability that he would take physical action during the event. But we wanted to find out if he was going to engage in a hostile collection of information (external or internal). We also wanted to prevent him, once inside, from opening up an unsanctioned access point (like one of the emergency egress doors) in order to allow his cohorts who were protesting outside to penetrate and disrupt the event.

For these reasons (and a few others), we deployed both external and internal covert field elements. Covertness in this case was important both for collecting the necessary field intelligence and also for maintaining appearances that would suit the organization's public relations needs.

The individual was first picked up by a covert SD operator in the Outer Circle, as soon as he neared the convention center where the event was taking place. He didn't engage in any external surveillance activities, and simply made his way to the entrance. This information was quickly relayed to our Inner Circle access control officers who did a very thorough job checking him through the metal detector gates (they even made him take his shoes off). The individual was then let into the venue where, unbeknownst to him, our covert internal security element (which I was a part of) kept him company during the entire event.

Intelligence will always have a certain cool, sexy aspect to it. When you see it in the movies, it's usually the intelligence gathering side that's glorified rather than the physical security end of things—where the intelligence actually gets implemented. But having been on both sides of this, I can say that there are few things more immediately satisfying than utilizing good, solid intelligence to get surgical, pin-pointed security results.

Up to this chapter, we've discussed a number of the key private security aspects—including intelligence, surveillance detection and physical protection. The topic of Circles of Security intentionally comes toward the end of the book because it puts these aspects into a single framework—allowing you to see how these various ingredients work together. The goal here was to take largely familiar situations (like attending a special event or entering a protected facility) and showcase some of the hard work that takes place behind the scenes—providing a unique look into a world that most people are unaware of.

CHAPTER 12

SO YOU WANT TO BE A COVERT OPERATOR

By this point in the book, some of you are bound to start asking how you, too, can get in on the action and become covert operators. So let me explain a few things about the work and what it's like, and if you're still interested, give you some pointers on how to get started.

WHAT IT'S LIKE

There's no denying that covert, special operations can be very interesting and even exciting at times. In fact, much of this book was dedicated to telling you about that. But if you want to understand what this work is really like, I should fill you in on the not-so-exiting parts as well.

Now, it's impossible to describe exactly what covert operations are like, if only because no two operations are the same. But here are two very common ingredients you're likely to find.

Tedium

Most operations have long stretches of time when nothing much is going on. I specifically chose the word *tedium* rather than boredom because despite the fact that not much is going on, you can never completely relax. It's only in retrospect that you can conclude nothing happened, but while you're still in it, no one's going to give you any warning if something comes up. In fact, you're the one who's supposed to detect it first and warn others about it. So even though absolutely nothing is happening the vast majority of time, you have to remain razor-sharp.

To get a tiny idea of what this can be like, picture a situation where you're covertly observing, say, an intersection from 5:00 am to 5:00 pm, for days on end, without detecting anything suspicious the entire time. Many people might assume (wrongly) that if a client was concerned enough to hire a surveillance detection or covert protection team, something dramatic must take place at a certain point. And though I have certainly had my share of dramatic moments, the majority of operations are long, tedious and drama-free.

Ambiguity

Considering how observant you have to remain when engaged in field intelligence operations, it's a bit ironic how little you actually learn. Even if you detect everyone in the area, it's quite unlikely you'll discover exactly *who* everybody was and *what* exactly they were up to. It's information that's simply not available to you. To make matters even more frustrating, you're often going to report your findings to a client who will investigate them but never let you know what they discovered. Even if your detections are reported to an intelligence and investigations department (*especially* if they're reported to a department like that), you're probably not going to hear back from them about their findings. There's no reciprocity when it comes to intelligence operations, and clients often have to contend with privacy, liability and disclosure issues that keep things on a need-to-know basis. The field operator is a source of data, not a consumer of intelligence. And though you might be very curious how things panned out, you'll often have to contend with not knowing.

WHAT IT TAKES

Though there are no formulas for what it takes to become a covert operator, here are a number of important factors that often come into play.

Heightened awareness:
By this I don't mean a heightened level of anxiety but rather an elevated level of visual awareness and careful observation. Maintaining these qualities is not only a function of using your eyes but of using what sits behind your eyes. It's a matter of concentration and attention to detail.

Now, I could tell you that this game is more of a marathon than a sprint, but a marathon only lasts around half a day or so while covert operations can go on for much longer than that. Anyone can maintain heightened awareness for short bursts, but can you maintain it for days on end? Which leads us to the next point.

Patience:
When an operator detects suspicious activity or hostile surveillance indicators, it might look like an exciting incident unfolded very quickly. But that would be a gross misrepresentation of where much of the operator's talent lies. If you've ever watched a documentary about magicians, you know that what looks like magic is the result of an insane amount of practice and preparation that preceded the execution of the trick. In much the same way, behind almost every interesting detection (from people surveilling the target to individuals flying small drones near a protected area) are days and days of tedium, tedium

which could have bored a less patient operator into complacency, preventing him/her from making the detection. Behind every molehill of a detection is a mountain of patience.

Discipline:
In the context of covert operations, discipline is the ability to accept and execute difficult instructions, even if you don't understand the reason behind them. This in no way means you have to always blindly accept orders. As in everything else, there's a balance to be struck. But in a secretive, complex, need-to-know type of environment, you're not always going to be given the full picture, and there are times when instructions simply need to be followed—no questions, arguments or explanations.

Self-discipline:
Self-discipline is your ability to execute the mission without cutting corners, to stick to it indefinitely even when you're not being supervised. Covert operators work alone most of the time, and, as I said earlier, much of the time nothing interesting is going on.

Imagine you're tasked with observing the abovementioned intersection for days on end, only your shift is 5:00 pm to 5:00 am. The temptation to start cutting corners at a certain point will be very strong. You might think that any decent operator would never compromise a mission for base, petty reasons, but I can tell you that being cold, tired, annoyed and burned out for days on end can really play with people's heads. And if you don't even think the role you're playing is an important one—that it's just a big waste of time and energy—the only thing that'll keep you going is self-discipline.

The ability to deal with ambiguity:
I touched on ambiguity in the section above. It's very often the case that you'll get instructions from your client or manager without getting a

satisfying explanation for why. Ordinarily, for conventional operations, this would not be a good thing. After all, we want every single operator to know as much as they can about the mission, the goals, who's involved in what, and what their methods of achieving their goals are. But we're not dealing with conventional operations here.

When it comes to unconventional operations, you very often have issues of privacy, operations security (OPSEC) and non-disclosure, which means information gets disseminated on a need-to-know basis. You'll have to be OK with the fact that your instructions might not always make perfect sense to you, that much of the big picture will be hidden from you, that you'll be giving much more information than you'll be receiving, and that no one owes you any explanations or follow-ups.

You'll have to also control your desire to find out how things panned out after a certain incident took place. You might be dying to know what happened with a certain suspicious person you reported on, especially after slaving for days until you made the detection. But it's considered very bad form to ask too many questions. If the client or manager didn't notify you, you should consider it as none of your business, and move on.

Self-reliance:
It's very often up to the operator to find tactical vantage points in the field, to establish a cover and cover story, to decide on various courses of action, and, most importantly, to adapt to unexpected situations. A field operator has to be a self-sufficient agent when the need arises, which it often does.

The ability to learn from mistakes:
I don't just mean this in the generic way that mistakes can be good learning opportunities. The SD and covert methodology learning process is practically based on your making mistakes. Causing you

to make these important mistakes and to experience failure is a big part of SD training. Accepting the fact that you made a mistake is not easy for most people (myself included), but having made so many of them, I can tell you that it's a vital ingredient in learning how to do things correctly.

Intelligence:
This is a big one and goes way beyond common sense. You have to be able to understand complex and ambiguous situations. You have to understand people and decipher the meaning and relevance behind what they're doing. You not only have to plan things intelligently, you have to react and adapt to unexpected situations in clever and inventive ways.

Self-reflection:
This is the ability to realize how you look, sound and feel to others around you. It's important for tactical reasons—to avoid calling attention to yourself as you blend into different environments—and it also comes into play when you communicate with a client.

It's common to find a lack of self-reflection in competitive, dominant people who transition from military, law enforcement or security work to sensitive, covert operations. In order to stop being a bull in a china shop, you'll have to first realize you've got big horns on your head. This is why training and learning from mistakes is so important, not just for understanding your environment but for understanding yourself.

Level-headedness and calm:
Last but not least, this might be the cornerstone that holds up all the other factors. Covert, special operations often contain many risks and potentially far-reaching consequences. You'll have a very hard time maintaining the factors mentioned above if you can't find a way to calm down and approach stressful situations in a level-headed way.

WHAT KIND OF PERSON CAN DO IT

The short answer here is that as long as they have the abovementioned qualities, anyone can do it. There's no single type of person or background that needs to fit any mold here. I've worked with people from many different walks of life who became successful at it, and many who didn't.

I suppose it's less surprising to discover that many of the people who excel at covert protective operations have military, law enforcement and security backgrounds. I've seen ex-Navy SEALs, ex-Secret Service agents and ex-undercover narcotics agents do amazing work. But some of my favorites (because they so beautifully go against conventions and common pre-expectations) are people who don't fit the classic mold. No disrespect to anyone with a strong military, law enforcement, government or security background (I have one of those myself), but it's always thrilling to see young Asian women, little old ladies and bicycle-riding hipsters run circles around ex-special forces guys in the field.

I touched on this topic in Chapter 9, but beyond appearance and demographics, what makes some of these people so great at covert operations is their flexible, unconventional open-mindedness. They still, of course, have to possess the qualities I mentioned earlier, but the bottom line is that there's no single type or character or background for this type of work. Different people with different backgrounds can all bring important and useful qualities to the table.

HOW TO GET STARTED

OK, so now that you've found out as much as you have about private sector covert operations and read all my warnings about it, if after all that you're still interested in getting into it for some odd reason, let me give you a few pointers on how to do it.

I can't really speak for the industry as a whole, nor can I guarantee that you'll succeed in getting into this field (most people don't), but I can tell you what it takes to work for me and a few others I know.

The number one thing you'll need is to gain your employer's trust. Many people miss this point, and I often get emails, messages and calls from people who throw their credentials at me, expecting to be immediately hired. Needless to say (or, unfortunately, not so needless), this is not the way it works.

Don't get me wrong, I'm not doubting anyone's skill and experience, but it takes a lot more than that. To take part in covert operations is to be brought very deeply into the fold, and clients and employers have to get to know you first. Skill and experience are necessary but not sufficient qualities on their own. There has to be a certain level of comfort and trust before "jumping into bed" together.

One way to get your foot in the door is to have a trusted insider vouch for you. This won't get you completely in but might kick-start the process. Another way to get started is to spend years working with someone like me on *conventional* protective operations. Then, after I get to know and trust you, we might take things to the next level. This can take quite a bit of time, which is another reason patience is an important virtue here.

In case you don't have any connections (and, actually, even if you do), training in surveillance detection and/or covert protection can also get things started. It's obviously vital for teaching inexperienced people the ropes. But even for people who already have some skill and experience, training is a low-stakes opportunity to show your employer what you're able to do and to get noticed and gain their trust.

Training is also an opportunity for the employer to see your specific brand and style of work. As I mentioned earlier, people from different backgrounds can bring different qualities to the table. But we, the employers, have to understand exactly what your qualities are and how they can be incorporated into our operations.

OK, you've almost made it to the end of the book. All we need now is to give you a few last important details, close things out and send you on your way.

CHAPTER 13

CONCLUSION

Palace Hotel, San Francisco. 2015 tech convention.

Remember our beleaguered CEO from the Introduction Chapter? The Silicon Valley executive who had been receiving increasingly violent threats from a particularly dedicated stalker? Well, as promised, here's the conclusion to that story.

As you may recall, the company's security director contacted me the night before the event to brief me on the situation and to ask if I would provide covert protective services for the CEO. At 6:00 am the next morning, I met the security director in the hotel lobby along with an additional operator I'd called in for the job. The three of us were dressed casually in order to fit into the crowd of 2,000 "techies" who would be arriving later that morning. We conducted a quick but thorough advance walk-through of the event space—including the conference area, the main stage, the private meeting rooms, and the exterior of the building.

Silicon Valley executives often make things quite tricky for their security details. This is because many of them don't want to think about security—let alone coordinate their movements with those in charge of protecting them—and this executive was a shining example of that. Much of the work we'd have to do was going to be unplanned. However, we prepared as best we could and coordinated with the CEO's driver and executive assistant to get a better idea of his schedule and movements.

Our plan was to avoid the busy main entrance and to direct the driver into an alley next to the hotel. From there, we'd get the CEO into the hotel through a side entrance, which led directly into the conference area. I took position outside the main entrance of the hotel, blending in with the tourists who were getting in and out of cabs. As the CEO's vehicle approached, I signaled to the driver to go down the alley until he reached the second operator who was waiting to escort the CEO into the building.

As the tech conference chugged along, we took various positions around the CEO. The second operator, who had provided executive protection to the CEO many times before, stayed as close as he could to him—joining his entourage on the conference floor and sitting in the front row when the CEO was on stage. I maintained a slightly farther distance—mingling with the attendees around the CEO on the conference floor and taking position backstage when he was on stage.

After his onstage appearance, we covertly escorted the CEO to a private meeting room which was one floor above the main conference area. As the meeting was coming to a close, however, we found ourselves in a bit of a dilemma. The CEO's meeting had run longer than expected, and his executive assistant informed us that he was already late for his next appointment back at the corporate headquarters.

While this wasn't exactly a security concern, the route we had planned for getting the CEO back to his vehicle would now need to change. It was originally supposed to take us back through the convention area and through a crowd of 2,000 techies—many of whom were waiting for the CEO with questions, pitches, and what have you. On top of that, there was an increased chance that the CEO's dangerous stalker would also make an appearance—particularly now that the twitterverse had been thoroughly updated about the CEO's presence at the conference. "We have to get him out fast," instructed the security director, "and I can't have him go down through that crowd."

A quick change of plan was in order. We decided to have the Close Protection operator escort the CEO to an emergency exit at the end of the upstairs corridor. From there, they would hurry down the dark staircase and out into the alley where the vehicle was waiting.

While this wasn't our original plan, we had covered this emergency exit route during our early morning walk-through. Realizing that we'd now need to utilize it, I quickly walked the route in advance—about two minutes before the CEO. When I got to the alley, I instructed the waiting driver to back up the vehicle so it was flush with the emergency door.

Within moments, the CEO was being driven away—leaving 2,000 attendees to wonder how in the world he had simply vanished.

FINAL THOUGHTS

So you've made it to the end of the book. Congratulations! Hopefully, it was fun, intriguing, and interesting; but is that all?

Well, not necessarily.

I obviously hope you've enjoyed the book, but if you've also learned a thing or two in the process, then, in a sense, you've also become a bit more capable. Of course, this doesn't mean you can now go out and engage in unconventional covert operations, just that you hopefully know a bit more about them. They say that knowledge is power, but I think it's more accurate (at least in this context) to say that knowledge is empowerment.

It might sound surprising, but many of the concepts I've covered in this book—even some of the sexier ones—can be applied in your own life as well. For example, the Circles of Security strategy we covered in Chapter 11 can be applied to your home. The surveillance detection and evasion principles we covered in Chapters 6, 7, and 10 can be applied to you and your loved ones. The inductive observation skills from Chapter 3 can be applied anytime and anywhere. It's all a question of which assets (people, property, and valuables) you care about and how you can better protect them. In essence, this is what all protective strategies are based on—so why not take some of that wisdom and apply it to the assets you yourself hold most dear?

The lessons shared in these pages are meant to raise your awareness and help you improve your own security. With that said, I'm not suggesting you start living your life in some paranoid security bubble. I certainly don't live my life that way. Knowing about the tactics used in covert operations doesn't mean you have to automatically implement them. But expanding your knowledge and raising your consciousness *can* help you make more informed decisions about your safety and security. For example, there's a reason why homes with burglar alarm stickers on their doors tend to have lower break-in rates. It's because hostile surveillants tend to scratch them off their potential target lists in favor of houses that seem easier (good idea to put some stickers on your doors).

There's also a reason why you tend to find more vehicle break-ins in areas where cars are parked in front of walls or large bushes rather than in front of private homes. These are areas where a hostile surveillant can operate with a lower risk of being detected (good idea to avoid parking your car overnight in front of a wall, bush, or empty lot).

Likewise, there's a reason why two personal friends of mine—on two separate occasions—had the trunks of their cars broken into, each losing a very valuable item. It appeared to them as a complete mystery. They didn't leave their cars parked for long, no other vehicles around had been broken into, and there was no way for the criminals to look into the trunks of their cars and see that a valuable item was hidden there. So how could the thieves have known which trunks to break into? The answer, of course, is that both of my friends had been covertly surveilled while they placed the expensive items in the trunks of their cars, since they both hid these items *after* arriving in the area and parking their cars. It wasn't luck—it was hostile surveillance that lead the thieves to those specific vehicles. (Incidentally, if you must store something in the trunk of your car, put it in there *before* you leave your current location, not after you park your car in a new area.)

There's also a reason why stalkers usually start by following their victims on social media, then close in on their victim's residence and workplace, and then begin following them to see where they go from there. This is a classic hostile planning process in which the hostile planner or stalker initially pulls their intel from readily available open sources before transitioning to static surveillance and then moving on to mobile surveillance.

I could keep going more or less indefinitely with examples like these—sharing advice on how to make better informed decisions—but the underlying messages would be the same: *Learn how to look at the world from different perspectives.* Understand how places and people (including yourself) can appear to potential hostile planners, and then change how you do things in order to shift the risk/benefit balance that a hostile planner uses to assess you. I know this might sound like highly technical, cloak-and-dagger kind of stuff, but the majority of defensive maneuvers and tactics (like the ones shared in the stories above) are almost laughably simple. And yet, just because they're simple doesn't mean everyone is born with innate knowledge about how to stay safe. Common sense is not always that common, at least not to those who never really stop to think about it. Remember the Sun Tzu quote from Chapter 1, "If you know the enemy and know yourself, you need not fear the result of a hundred battles."

Speaking of common, it's at this point that I often get one of the more predictable objections to educating people about surveillance, surveillance detection, and protective operations. Aren't I helping the "bad guys" by teaching them how to surveil? Aren't I also informing them of how security works, and therefore, on how to bypass our protective efforts? Well, the answer to the first question is that the bad guys don't usually need much help when it comes to surveillance. They're the ones who already know how it works. In my experience, it's the good guys who are mostly in the dark about it (since they've never had any reason to think about it or experience it). Not to denigrate my professional field, but it's not exactly rocket science. Acquiring the skills is mostly a matter of raising your consciousness and sensitivity and gaining some experience in it—things that most bad guys have already done. Now it's your turn to catch up.

As for the second question, the answer is also no. Equipping a hostile planner with general knowledge about protective operations doesn't really help them bypass or evade security measures (as long as the information isn't too specific). This is because general knowledge about a target doesn't eliminate the need for the hostile planner to eventually show up in the area of the target (in order to collect more detailed information). It's at this point that we, as security professionals, can detect, acknowledge, or investigate the hostile threat.

One of the most empowering things to learn about crime and criminals is how relatively vulnerable they are during their planning and surveillance stages, and how relatively simple it is to detect and deter them once you understand how things work. These vulnerabilities are inherent in the nature of crime and cannot simply be overcome or bypassed by knowing a bit more about security. Again, the bad guys already know this since they're the ones who are experienced in balancing high-risk situations. The good guys are the ones who need to catch up on what's going on around them.

As interesting as you might have found some of the cases I discussed in this book, they pale in comparison to other operations I've taken part in, and to some of the ones my friends and colleagues have been through (which I'm not at liberty to share). My own experiences are by no means unique, nor am I the best out there—far from it. I'm just the guy who was kind enough to hand you this limited-access backstage pass.

I hope this book has opened your eyes to a few new things and that it might change your perspective on the world. As you've seen, things are often not what they seem. Tourists, corporate employees, hotel workers, registered convention attendees, or any average person walking down the street or sitting in a coffee shop could be a covert operator on the job. I can say this with confidence because I myself have "been" all these people, so to speak.

In the introduction to this book, I promised to tell you about the Surveillance Zone, and show you where it is. Now that you've gotten to the end of the book, the answer to where it is should be quite obvious. It's all around you—it always has been. In fact, I can almost guarantee that you yourself have, without knowing it, been an audience member or even an extra on numerous occasions when protective operations or covert field exercises were taking place.

So the next time you're out and about, give the hardworking covert protective operators out there a polite nod of the head. Don't expect any of us to nod back, but depending on where you happen to be, you can definitely expect us to see it.

Acknowledgments   There are a great many people I'd like to thank for sticking with me over the years, and for playing a part in the writing of this book. The mentors who've taught me, the clients who've hired me, the operators I've recruited, trained and managed, the dedicated professionals who've toiled in the trenches with me. Though most of you must remain nameless, please know that I am eternally grateful.

Thank you to all the readers who have stuck with me over the years.

And last but not least, I want to extend a special thank you to Sammy Joselewitz and to Ivor Terret.

Made in the USA
San Bernardino, CA
27 December 2019